Politics of Protection

By the Same Author

1. Dalit in Action
2. Elite and Development (with Sachchidananda)
3. Protective Discrimination: Ideology and Praxis
4. Secularism: Concept and Practice
5. Social Exclusion: Essays in Honour of Dr. Bindeshwar Pathak (In 2 Volumes)
6. Urban Family (The): A Study of Hindu Social System

About the Author

Prof. A.K. Lal is a Sociologist. He started his career from A.N. Sinha Institute of Social Studies, Patna. He held positions of eminence and contributed impressively on various themes of sociological interest. As Head, Political Science Division he conducted important studies on shifting locus of power in Bihar. His book "Politics of Poverty" received widespread appreciations. Prof. Lal has also been a Senior Fellow at G.B. Pant Social Science Institute, Allahabad. He was a Senior Fellow of the Indian Council of Social Science Research, New Delhi. His areas of interest include study of the weaker sections especially the Scheduled Castes, changing contours of rural India, role of third sector initiatives in addressal of deficits of development. Prof. Lal has authored/edited many important books. His research articles have found inclusion in professional journals.

Politics of Protection

A Study of Other Backward Classes in Bihar

A.K. Lal

CONCEPT PUBLISHING COMPANY PVT. LTD.
NEW DELHI-110059

ISBN-13: 978-93-86682-47-5

First Published 2019

Published and Printed by

Since 1974

Concept Publishing Company Pvt. Ltd.
A/15-16, Commercial Block, Mohan Garden,
New Delhi-110059 (India)
T : 91 11 25351460, 91 11 25351794
E : publishing@conceptpub.com, *W*: www.conceptpub.com

Cataloging in Publication Data--Courtesy: D.K. Agencies (P) Ltd. <docinfo@dkagencies.com>

Lal, A. K., author.
Politics of protection : a study of other backward classes in Bihar / A.K. Lal.
pages cm
Includes bibliographical references and index.
ISBN 9789386682475

1. Caste—Political aspects—India—Bihar. 2. Reverse discrimination—India—Bihar. 3. Social mobility—India—Bihar. 4. Bihar (India)—Politics and government. I. Title

LCC DS422.C3L35 2019 | DDC 305.560954123 23

Preface

The study of the Other Backward Classes movement represents an important concern among the social scientists. Scholars interested in identifying the facets of social change have evinced keen interest in analysis of the responses of the people from this section towards the forces of economic growth, social mobilisation and democratization. We have materials for different periods in diverse contexts that illustrate the stresses and strains encountered in the wake of rising aspirations for upward mobility in a society in transition. Attempts to integrate available materials on the changing status of the middle range castes in different settings provide impressive insights. In spite of this, there are areas and dimensions that have failed to receive the attention they merit. Updating the information already accumulated has to acquire priority in order to describe the latest. While some work on the Other Backward Classes of Bihar has been done, these discuss only the fringe of the problem. The present book, however, seeks to explore in depth as well as in coverage the initiatives of the middle range castes of Bihar to lift themselves in socio-economic hierarchy. Special treatment has been given to their emergence as locus of power in the State. Our concern has been to provide insights to the extent and direction of change in the status of Other Backward Classes in Bihar.

The book is the outcome of the study that I perused as Senior Fellow of the Indian Council of Social Science Research, New Delhi. I am grateful to the Council for the honour and financial support. My son, Kumar Abhishek, deserves praise for his computer support. I wish him happy and prosperous future.

Samriddhi, my lovely daughter, has been a source of inspiration and spiritual support. She read the manuscript thoroughly and offered suggestions for my considerations. My wife, who was perhaps the happiest person on my new position and assignment, spared me from some of the urgent concerns of the family and willingly shouldered the responsibilities that should otherwise have been my exclusive concern. I have a desire to have her support in future also and wish to keep her happy with my academic works. Shri Ashok Kumar Mittal, Concept Publishing Company Pvt. Ltd., is a fond member of my extended family. He is a worthy son of a worthy father from whom he inherited qualities that sustain him in this profession with dignity. I owe to him a deep sense of gratitude for his many acts of kindness. This book is dedicated to the memory of my aunt, Late Smt. Sheo Kumari Devi, for her kind financial support to get me enrolled for the post-graduate studies. I offer my sincere homage and wish her soul a peaceful rest.

13.2.2018 **A.K. Lal**
Mahashivaratri

Contents

Preface v

1. Introduction 1
2. The Other Backward Classes in Bihar 10
3. Quest for Mobility: An Analysis of Other Backward Classes Movement in the Historical Perspective 29
4. Empowerment Through Protective Discrimination 49
5. The Other Backward Classes Under One Party Dominance System 71
6. The Other Backward Classes as Locus of Power 88
7. Summary and Conclusions 107

Appendices

1. The OBC Population according to the First Backward Classes Commission 115
2. The Population of 17 Major Castes and their Relative Share in the Total Population of Bihar as a whole in 1931 Census 116
3. Caste Composition of the Members of the Bihar State Legislative Assembly (1967-2000) 117
4. Caste Composition of the Lok Sabha Members from Bihar, 1952-2004 118
5. Social Composition of President and Secretaries at the District Level 119

6. Caste of Candidates for Bihar Assembly Elections, 1995 120

7. Caste Background of Chairmen, Members of Zilla Parishads and Mukhias in Bihar 2001 121

8. Position in Some Important Centres in Bihar 122

9. Caste and Community of Members of Janta Dal Governments in Bihar 123

Index 124

1

Introduction

Such sections of society that represent the social space between upper castes and untouchables have been initiator of unprecedented change in India. The traditional inferiors under the leadership of individuals from the stratum afflicted to 'inequality of the second order' resisted the inherited and ordained. Social pedigree as resource of mobility was unacceptable as attribution of inequality of status based on birth was forcefully negated. Claims for superior location in the traditional stratification system were made in the initiatives of the status-deprived of attributes of status ensuring dominance of the section located at the apex of the stratification system. Wedded to weakening of inequality embedded in tradition these castes made systematic strivings for removal of the obsolete and irrelevant. Such castes subsequently used their federative strength and numerical spread to acquire impressive location in society.

Opposition to the fixed location of the ritually superior manifested in an incline on the part of the middle range castes to evolve a social order that emphasized truth reason and equality as its ideological components. Intolerable religious impositions were unacceptable as individual conscience and reason were considered the best guide to spiritual progress. Organisation and education were considered essential for attainment of such goals. The ritual dominance and cultural pre-eminence of the numerically sparse superiors in the hierarchy encountered resistance in the ideological stirrings of the middle range castes as they federated themselves to seek redemption from the dominance of the 'fastidious and isolated'. Institutionalisation and coherence characterised such upsurge. Successful mobilization of these people led to erosion in the hold of the entrenched in politics bureaucracy and professions.

Struggle for equality with the superior in the social hierarchy acquired other dimensions also. Claims of parity with the 'clean' at the apex in the caste hierarchy found expression in the middle castes' initiatives for anticipatory socialization to the culture of the superiors. *Shudra's* unease thus found expression in stirrings aimed at inner reform to claim *'dwija'* status. Traditionally legitimised rituals and ideologies and markers of superior status turned out to be the reference model for emulation. Claims of superior lineage, however, turned to be weak facilitator for status elevation. Such stirrings for cultural mobility instead of serving the interest intended fostered the traditionally ordained framework. Instincts for equality with the upper castes ushered a divide among the middle range castes making it difficult for them to seek the demise of the embedded. Soft and conciliatory opposition to inherited disability eluded these castes space proximate to the upper castes in spite of their willingness to appropriate 'traditional' symbol of honour. The intermediate castes waited at the periphery as the prevalent social equilibrium and intrasegementary cleavages thwarted their attempts for ascendance. Inertia and orientation to succourance needs forced them to affiliate themselves with the upper caste outfits.

Strategies for the upward mobility of the other backward classes in some cases have emphasized the acquisition of modern attributes of status. Oriented to removal of inherited inferiority the status order comprising the clean among the inferiors pressed for their inclusion in the state's list for protection and support. Socio-economic development and consequent resource endowment favoured such aspirations. Consolidation of force in middle of the hierarchy of caste, however, turned out to be most impressive in the wake of their struggle for entitlement of benefits under the scheme for protective discrimination. Their initiatives to seek enlargement of the ambit of protective discrimination led to a situation that warranted the immediate federation of disaggregated among the status deprived *shudras*.

Identically placed status group coalesced to acquire wider space and effective presence in the emerging stratification system. "New possibilities inherent in universal suffrage and proposals for reservation" led them to shift their strategy for mobility "outside the caste system by capturing state power". Inclusiveness witnessed in wake of opposition to the initiatives for their sponsored inclusion in the bureaucracy enabled them to aggregate and integrate electoral and interest group support. Their success in this regard ushered an unprecedented transformation in the elite structure favouring extended space for the section thus raised. Social diversity acquired increased incorporation in the elite structure as congruence thus arrived led to a situation of dispersed dominance. Its impact tended to be rapid and effective as it led to unprecedented erosion in the power of the embedded. As social pedigree lost its importance as resource of power the intermediate castes appeared least interested in acquisition of relative superiority within the ritual hierarchy.

Initiatives made and strategies adopted in the attempts made for mobility of the other backward classes have been the theme of several studies. Social situation and leadership involved in such stirrings have been accorded scholarly scrutiny. Crusade against inequalities enshrined in the social order has received sociological attention. The studies on the non-*brahmanic* movements have elaborated the role of the middle range castes as prime movers in stirrings for elevation in the status of the deprived sections. As leaders of the movements challenging the assumption and attribution of inequality based on birth these castes made concerted efforts to weaken the fetters of tradition imposing restrictions on the mobility of the low in the hierarchy. Studies on non-*Brahmin* movements represented 'the first point' in the upsurge of the peasant castes and have produced substantive knowledge on the phenomenon of change and continuity in the caste system. Such studies have uncovered the modalities and ramifications of protest and assertion of sections oriented to change in the traditional arrangement.[1] *Shudras'* mobilisation that subsequently led to unprecedented shift in locus of power in favour of these castes has also received attention in the works of eminent social scientists. Studies on their endeavours to seek elevation in the traditional stratification system as well as their success in acquisition of economic prosperity and political empowerment have been accorded priority attention in works discussing change and continuity in the social system. Attempts have been made to explore the implications of planned development and diversification in the modern occupational structure on the social and political status of the castes comprising this category. Shah has detailed the studies that seek to analyse the cases where the middle range castes have resorted to sanskritization as strategy for status elevation. It is maintained that this endogenous and culture specific source of social change has found favour mostly with the economically prosperous and politically conscious sections among the intermediate castes. Status characteristics of the leaders of such movements, the institutionalization of their programmes for reconstruction of the society and modalities of support recruitment constitute the theme of enquiry in these works.[2] Studies have also been made to discuss the rise of particular castes from among such castes in terms of their political efficacy indicating resilience of federative cohesion as an important means for attainment of sectional interest. Empirical and theoretical findings thus made available provide clues for explorations on political development and social change among these castes. Strategies in such initiatives find elaborations in the studies investigating increased consciousness and aroused aspirations of these castes.[3]

Contexts that manifested impulses for elevated location in the social order and share in the secular resources much after the non-*Brahmin* movements have also been studied.[4] Explorations on rise of kulak picked the thread left in studies made earlier on the role of middle caste peasants in seeking freedom from the colonial exploitation.[5] The work on social conflicts that ensued in the wake of commercialization of agriculture brings into sharp focus the contradictions involved in the rise of these bullock captalists.[6] Sponsored politicization of such castes find articulation in some other works on changing contours of power structure. Distortion in formation and implementation of measures of protective discrimination crept on account of the selfish aims of manipulative interests among the other backward classes is a priority concern in studies on the rise of these castes in the wake of the *mandalisation* of politics. Weighted index of backwardness is suggested to be evolved to ensure a better fit between deprivation and protective support.[7] Checks and balances are recommended for inclusion in the social policy in this regard to stem distortions.[8] Works representing sociological critique of the equality provisions through the extension of reservation discourage unethical and motivational support to legitimise biases and prejudices in favour especially through manipulated research and caution is suggested to be taken to ensure sincerity of purposes in the intentions of the state in this regard.[9] Competing commitments in favour of reservation is said to ignore the costs and ineffectiveness involved. Stresses and strains triggered in the wake of opportunistic extension to the provisions of compensatory preferences are other dimension deserving attention require proper attention.[10] Studies on changing contours of political representation especially in the states that have been witness to the second wave of the rise of the middle range castes offer insightful understanding with regard to success and constraints in the rise of this section of society. The studies reveal that while inner contradictions within the intermediate castes continue, their rise in politics has led to decline in the power of the upper castes. Such situation, it is pointed out, favours the empowerment of the Scheduled Castes also as they are equally opposed to the political rehabilitation of the upper castes.[11] Summing up, the discussion on the review of literature available on the theme of the other backward classes it can be said that it represents an important concern among the social scientists. Scholars interested in identifying the facets of social change seem to have evinced keen interest in the analysis of the responses of the people from these castes towards the forces of economic growth, social mobilization and democratization. We have materials for different periods in diverse contexts on identical dimensions. Attempts to integrate the available materials on the changing status of the middle range castes in different social settings provide impressive insights. There is, however, a need for more work as many situations remain unexplored. Updating of the information already available is required to know the latest.

Contemporary Bihar represents a situation where the recently forged middle castes' unity has produced profound political consequences. Struggle for availability of benefits of reservation has stirred them to federate themselves to acquire unprecedented political aggregation. It marks the inauguration of a phase of political renaissance, a watershed and ensures wide integration among the intermediate castes. The present power structure in the state is loaded in favour of the Other Backward Classes.[12] Consolidated into a conscious political force these have weakened the hold of tradition as resource of power. Inducted recently in political arena the erstwhile excluded and non-privileged now acquire a location that was earlier denied to them. Context favourable to perpetuation of the dominance of the upper castes has undergone transformation. The middle range castes have emerged effective replacement to the embedded feudals. The themes in the protest ideology of the middle range castes constitute priority areas for exploration as these provide clues to the understanding of change and continuity in the traditional stratification system. The present study is devoted to the exploration of the context and consequences of the rise of the intermediate castes in Bihar. Their role as forces wedded to reduction of inequality is sought to be detailed. Nature of core and support involved in such protest initiatives are analysed. Efforts to seek upward placement in the traditional hierarchy as well as endeavours to arrange effective fit between development and equality constitute its concern. Conditions conducive to socio-political unity of such sections have been accorded detail scrutiny. Situations inimical to sustenance of solidarities thus forged have been studied in historical perspective to explain propensity for splits. Scope and limits of different mobility strategies favouring empowerment of the other backward classes have been outlined. Attempts have been made to identify the reference group for identification and emulation and also the negative reference group in initiatives. The role of paracommunities is studied to assess their effectiveness in interest articulation and pressure group formation. Accommodative capacity of the consociational arrangement and stresses and strains produced in the wake of competing interests of diverse interests comprising the congeries constitute other themes for exploration. Support as well as opposition to such endeavours from outside the configuration have been detailed to obtain rounded perspective on the phenomenon. We have discussed the factors responsible for disturbing traditional congruence of attributes of status. Our aim has been to elaborate the nature and consequences of initiatives made to seek a replacement favouring forces on ascendance. The following constitutes the detail objectives of the study:

- to prepare a socio-economic profile of the middle range castes in the state of Bihar;

- to describe in detail the extent of similarities and differentiations among the castes comprising this category;
- to study the impact of schemes for economic growth and operation of forces of political modernization in promotion of their economic prosperity and political empowerment;
- to analyse the representation of the other backward classes in power structure to facilitate understanding of change and continuity in the structure of dominance;
- to discuss in detail the role of political parties and para-communities in sponsoring mobility of the castes comprising this social category;
- to study in depth as well as in coverage the initiatives of these castes for claiming rank elevation in the traditionally legitimised social order;
- to describe in detail the extent and pattern of resistance encountered by them from the forces opposed to attainment of their rising aspirations;
- to obtain an understanding of the context that spurred them to resist traditionally perpetuated dominance and denial of their due in the emerging opportunity structure;
- to delineate the pattern of relationship between the middle range castes and the Scheduled Castes in the past and at the present so as to indicate the direction of change in the society;
- to analyse the impact of the existence and operation of forces wedded to radical socio-economic transformation on the caste based solidarity fostered among the middle range castes; and
- to attempt presentation of hypotheses on changing pattern of status mobilization of the intermediate castes in comparative perspective.

The work is a contribution to the growing literature on the theme of 'the Other Backward Classes'. We have treated this social category as a social unit to explore and analyse it as a complex whole. Our endeavour has been to attempt an inclusive and intensive examination of different facets related to changing contours of social reality with special reference to the status of the other backward classes. Support materials for the study have been culled out from the available literature on the dimensions comprising the outlines seeking attention in the study. We collected information available in different reports on this section of society to describe the reality. Newspaper reports have details on stirrings seeking corporate status mobility. Information is also available on federative initiatives among the proximate in the social order in journals of repute. Data on impact of implementation of recommendation of the commissions are available in the documents of the State Government. Gleanings on changing representation of these castes in the institutions of power have to be found in the reports of the Election Commission. Para-communities have institutionalised existence. Their aims, activities, programmes and impact may be known from the materials available with them. We have collected relevant information from such documents and integrated them to obtain meaningful insights. Content analysis have been resorted to process relevant information from the available documents with the aim to ensure systematic understanding. We have interviewed political leaders, social activists, journalists, and bureaucrats also. Raw materials thus made available constitute the basis for interpreting the facets that are the priority concern of the study.

REFERENCES

1. See Eugene F. Irschick, (1969), *Politics and Social Conflict in South India,* Oxford University Press, Bombay; M.S. Gore, (1989), *Non-Brahman Movement in Maharashtra.* Segment Book Distributors, New Delhi; M.S. Gore, (1989), "Social Movements and the Paradigm of Functional Analysis" in *Economic and Political Weekly* Vol. 14. No. 17; H.F. Owen, (1987), "The non-*Brahmin* Movements and the Transformation of Congress 1921-22", in *Struggling and Ruling,* (ed.) by Jim Masselos, Sterling Publishers Pvt. Ltd., New Delhi.
2. Ghanshyam Shah, (1990), *Social Movement in India,* Sage Publications India Pvt. Ltd., New Delhi.
3. Robert L., Hardgrave, Jr., (1968), *The Nadars of Tamil Nadu: The Political Culture of a Community in Change,* University of California Press, Berkeley; also *see* Lioyd I. Rudolph, Susanne Hoebler Rudolph, (1987), *The Modernity of Tradition,* Orient & Longman, New Delhi.

4. M.S.A. Rao, (1978), *Social Movements and Social Transformation in India,* Macmillan, New Delhi.
5. L.I. Rudolph and Susanne H. Rudolph, (1984), "Determinants and Varieties of Agrarian Mobilisation" in *Agrarian Power Agricultural Productivity in South Asia,* (ed.) by Meghnad Desai *et al.,* Oxford University Press, New Delhi.
6. *See* for such information especially on Bihar L.I. Rudolph and S.H. Rudolph, (1989), In *Pursuit of Lakshmi,* Orient Longman Limited, Hyderabad; Francine R. Frankel, (1993), "Caste, Land and Dominance in Bihar", in Francine R. Frankel and M.S.A. Rao, *Dominance and State Power in Modern India,* Vol. 1, Oxford University Press, New Delhi; Pradhan H. Prasad, (1979), "Semi-feudalism: the basic constraints of Indian agriculture", in Arvind N. Das and V. Nilkant, *Agrarian Relations in India,* Manohar, New Delhi.
7. A.K. Lal, (2002), "Protective Discrimination: Social Necessity or Political Compulsions," in A.K. Lal *Protective Discrimination: Ideology and Praxis,* Concept Publishing Company, New Delhi.
8. G. Thimmaiah, (1993), *Power Politics and Social Justice: Backward Castes in Karnataka,* Sage Publications, New Delhi.
9. Andre Bettelie, (1992), *The Backward Classes in Contemporary India,* Oxford University Press, Bombay; S.R. Maheshwari, (1991), *The Mandal Commission and Mandalisation,* Concept Publishing Company, New Delhi.
10. Marc Galenter, (1984), *Competing Equalities,* Oxford University Press, New Delhi.
11. Harry W. Blair, (1980), "Rising Kulaks and Backward Classes in Bihar", *Economic and Political Weekly,* Vol. 15, No. 21; A.K. Lal, (1995), "Segmented Pluralism: A Study of Caste, Politics and Assembly Elections in Bihar", *Mainstream,* March 11; A.K. Lal, *Nemesis,* Seminar 1979.
12. A.K. Lal, (1996), "Caste and Politics in Bihar: a study of 1995 elections", *Journal of Social and Economic Studies.*

2

The Other Backward Classes in Bihar

'Other Backward Classes' constitutes a 'giant new category of the collectively deprived.'[1] Called earlier as backward classes the term 'other backward classes' is an 'administrative euphemism'[2] for the castes "whose ritual rank and occupational status was above the untouchables but in the lower reaches of the caste order of traditional society."[3] The term is preferred to 'backward castes' in deference to a desire on the part of India's secular modernising national leadership to diminish the importance of caste or to do away with the caste distinctions entirely.'[4] The category was "developed to identify those who are not specifically mentioned in the Constitution under the schedules which specify the Scheduled Castes and Tribes".[5] It is thus a constitutional category representing a social layer intermediate between the 'twice-born' on the one hand and the untouchables on the other. Such sections are inferior to the upper castes not only ritually but also educationally and economically. Constrained by the inequality legitimised under the traditional stratification system they have been rendered inferior to the socially privileged. Caste system kept them oppressed in spite of the fact that they were neither isolated nor despised. The term connotes a "status order defined by traditional (*dharmic*) ritual ranking of castes and the state's official sociology of the disadvantaged communities."[6]

The castes comprising the other backward classes differ from each other. Social backwardness does not confer same status to different castes. The category includes different classes comprising the rural economy. Large landowners from the better-off middle range castes to numerous agricultural labourers from such castes and also from the most backward castes are included. Class differentiation is sharp as in addition to a thin crust of powerful landowners there is significant presence of owner peasants, landless wage earners and sharecroppers ploughing small pieces of land. Extremely depressed castes such as artisans and servicing castes are clubbed together with land owning castes with superior lineage. Castes thus federated for economic support and social enlistment include the 'bullock capitalists' brought into existence on account of the implementation of the policies of land reforms and the measures oriented to the supply of inputs for intensive agricultural development and comprise also those whom these beneficiaries of the first wave of sponsored agrarian development denied the succour of special packages as marginal farmers and landless labourers.

These middle range caste peasantry prospered more than the large land holders in the upper castes. Such sections were more effective in taking advantage of the benefits of planned agricultural development. The expanding market for their agricultural produces and diary products increased their earnings. They were no longer required to make unnecessary payments to the landlords as the *zamindari* system was abolished. Their direct involvement in agriculture and proneness to accept innovations in agriculture constituted the other factors contributing to their economic betterment. Earnings from these sources were not spent on acquisition of luxuries. These were invested in new ventures. This was evident from large land transfers to these sections from the upper castes. In some of the areas they invested their newly acquired income to start cold storages and cinema houses. Some of them turned out to be influential transport operators. While resisting the oppressive upper castes these upper *shudras* whose commercial impulses enabled to profit from the state initiatives for rural development are intolerant to the rising aspirations of the Scheduled Castes also often surpassing the upper castes in cruelty. The owner cultivators from the middle range castes are autonomous entrepreneurs unlike the "umbrella farmers from the upper castes' and are ruthless exploiters prone to 'drive their agricultural labourers very hard."[7] These like the upper caste feudals oppose wage structure for their labourers. Their prosperity that was possible on account of the rise in the price of the agricultural commodities has ensured a wide cleavage between them and the landless agricultural labours and non-cultivating land owners. Once exploited by the upper castes they appear to betray similar insensitivity to the interests of poorer sections in the production system including the poor from the middle range castes. Kulaks find themselves closer to feudals than to the labourers. Poor and low, therefore, suffer from cumulative disadvantages. Landlessness, non-availability of marketable skills, sharp internal divisions and low numerical strength make them economically dependent and politically weak. These extremely backward castes comprise people of "even more disparate livelihoods, statuses and economic circumstances" than the scheduled population. The components comprising the category thus are differentially located in the stratification system. Land is unevenly distributed among them. Owner cultivators are mostly found among the top few. Lower to them and more numerous are the castes which are landless tenant cultivators, artisans and service castes who remain under the economic and political control of the land owning castes. In the past they had to work as forced labourers, domestic servant and *palanquin* bearers for those upon whom they depended for their survival. Placed as *shudras* the other backward classes thus spans a wide "cultural and structural arch" comprising the landowning dominant castes as well as castes with status proximate to the socio-economic status of the untouchables. Taking cue from such diversity attempts are made to classify the castes included under two separate categories of upper *shudras* and lower *shudras*. Such middle range castes which are economically well off and occupy important position in the power structure are labelled as the upper *shudras* while those at the margin of subsistence and politically insignificant are termed as the lower *shudra*. The upper *shudras* have most of the 'bullock capitalists' from the middle range castes. In Bihar the upper *shudras* constitute 11 per cent of the state population while the lower *shudras* account for 29 per cent of the population of the state.

Since the people comprising this social category never suffered untouchability and isolation they are described as a stratum of non-untouchables Hindu castes that are socially and economically inferior and are placed in the middle of the stratification system. This notwithstanding social uniformity among the components comprising the other backward classes is unnatural. It is an imposition, a reconstruction, to make inferiority the basis for claiming state support. Politically this label for the middle range castes has facilitated construction of subaltern identity on caste lines.

The other backward classes have substantive presence in Bihar. They are numerically the most dominant section of its population.[8] These are placed in the middle of the stratification system and most of them had to encounter socio-economic disabilities in the past. Cumulative resource disadvantages made most of the middle range castes exclusively dependent on the upper castes for their survival. They survived on the meagre payments that they received from these land owning castes for their services. Such social contexts had traditionally legitimised arrangements favouring the upper castes. Economic exploitation of such castes used to be institutionalised under the *jajmani* system. Loan to persons in distress and that too on unfavourable terms forced the debtor to work in the field of the money lender in lieu of the interests that was supposed to be paid. Short duration arrangement soon tended to get converted into life long relationship. There used to be instances where the inability to pay back the loan with interests resulted in transfer of the burden to the family members in the next generation. There were many areas where without loan bonded labourers mainly from the Scheduled Castes were made available to the upper castes. Such favours were available to the upper castes under a traditionally sanctioned mechanism known as the *kamiauti* system where the landowning upper castes and landless land tilling exterior castes were attached to each other in a life long stable alliance. The system of bondage thus prevalent as a component of the caste system tended to be hereditary regulating the relationship between patrilineal descent groups of masters and servants. As an institution of fairly long standing, it represented a channel or conduit to transfer rights and obligations from one generation to another. *Kamiauti* arrangements permitted sale and mortgage of the labourers, if so warranted, as if they were transferable commodity.

Large section of the poor among the middle range castes had to depend on the upper castes not only out of economic necessity but also on account of the fact that the tradition sanctioned such dependence. Under the arrangement that governed the inter-personal relationship among the different castes the low has to be inferior to the castes claiming superior pedigree. Castes tended to be socially distant occupying graded location in the stratification system. Qualitative restrictions on consumption and behaviour prevailed. Status disabilities restricted the nature of dress the lower castes were permitted to don. Seating on cot in presence of upper castes, use of footwear and umbrella in the streets, where the people from upper castes resided, were intolerable as the lower castes were not supposed to have these 'privileges'. There was little resistance on the part of the lower castes against such treatment as even unintentional violation of the 'established pattern' was meted with severe punishment. The low caste people were also not permitted to name their children in the manner they desired. Some names reserved for the upper castes were not available for the sons and daughters of the lower caste families. Such mechanisms nurtured instincts of submission in the lower castes and facilitated their unrestrained acquiescence to the upper castes. The values internalised under this system of hierarchical submission entailed upon the lower castes the 'solemn duty' to serve the superiors in the hierarchy. Services received from the upper castes not only violated the tradition but was also considered sinful. Upper castes considered themselves socially privileged to humiliate the womenfolk from the lower castes. Women from the poor lower caste families were subjected to sexual abuse. The upper castes considered it to be their prerogative. It was almost 'a tradition' completing 'a picture of unbridled overlordship' of the upper castes.[9] Under the *dola* system such sexual exploitation tended to be institutionalised making it obligatory on the part of the newly married woman from the weaker sections to submit herself first to the village landlord to satisfy his lust. Under this arrangement there were places where upper caste women were also not spared but that used to be exceptional as it was more applicable in the cases of lower castes. There were till recently places where women from these castes used to be supplied to the upper castes individuals on rates fixed by the *lathait* of the landlord. Probably no society in the world accords such latitude to the privileged section. Education tended to be sparse among such section of society not only because they lacked the resources, but also because the upper castes did not like them to be educated. Instances are reported where punishments were meted to the boy from lower castes for doing better in examinations than their upper castes colleagues.

These and many more similar practices used to provide extra-economic coercion to lull the lower castes people into deep slumber of inertia and inaction and to enable the upper castes to keep them in a state of complete dependence on them. Thus, in Bihar socially inferior had to endure different forms of humiliations. They were not supposed to question indignities that perpetuated. The location of a caste in the stratification system used to fix the scope of privileges that the caste in question was entitled while interacting with other castes. It also used to determine the extent and pattern of subordination. Attempts to resist exploitation did not have the endorsement of the society. Violations of the prevalent code regulating interpersonal relationship led to serious repercussions. Often the privileged and ritually superior treated the communities lower to them in the stratification system as their personal property commanding total control not only over them but also over their entire family.

Under the permanent settlement introduced to ensure collection of revenue from the villages the *raiyats* mostly from the lower castes had to encounter grievous oppression under the *zamindars* who operated as intermediary between the peasants and the colonial rulers. This system reinforced the congruence of caste with class legitimised under the pervasive traditional social order. The upper castes as well as high status Muslims were prosperous land owners and most of the big *zamindars* and small landlords belonged to this section of society. The *zamindari* system tended to be exploitative as well as discriminatory. It was unfair to the lower castes. Peasants from the lower castes had to pay more than their counterparts in the upper castes. The duration of tenure used to be short in the case of the ritually inferior. It was customary for the low caste people to work as unpaid labourers. Different generic names were used for the tenants of different castes. Separate places of living ensured insularity to the twice-born from the sight and touch of the unclean. Peasants from the artisan castes were also required to render services free of cost and had to ensure free supply of the materials manufactured by them to the landlords. Even the Scheduled Castes with specialised skills were not spared. On many occasions lower caste peasants were forced to work without any payment. Under the colonial rule the lower castes were the worst sufferers as they lost their land and status. The untouchables were in a amore deplorable state living in insularity and surviving on the leftovers. The *zamindari* system not only made the intermediaries prosperous but also favoured their employees especially the keepers of the land records who conspired with them by distorting the land records and thus enabling them in appropriation of the lands of others. In course of time these record keepers became so rich that some of them turned out to be landlords. The members of such families were the first to evince interest in western education and were also the initial entrant in the state services. Upper caste landed aristocracy in control of power and bureaucracy ensured 'calm and order' in the society. The low and exploited had to be passive and inert as the political leadership tended to be oppressive and the bureaucracy indifferent. Such contexts of dominance did not favour reform in agrarian structure In spite of being ideologically wedded to support peasant movements the Congress did not allow peasant unrest to spread to the extent these deserved. So long the peasants opposed the European planters or the British Government their initiatives had the endorsement and support of the Congress. The party did not, however, evince interest in uprisings with the potential of threatening the perpetuation of *status quo* in the rural power structure. The 'petty landlords, the middle class urban professionals having stakes in land and rich peasants' comprising the leadership of the organisation were cautious to prevent shift in power favouring the rising aspirations.[10] The context thus prevalent has been described as 'multi-stranded' representing the 'ideal type' where various attributes of status congrued to ensure superiority to the section placed at the apex of the stratification. Traditionally legitimised the privileged location of the upper castes in the social structure received endorsement in the colonial arrangements for governance.

Numerical superiority of the middle range castes was not considered a threat to the dominance of the upper castes on account of their economic inferiority. In "the structure of subinfeduation that built up over years of British rule" the upper castes possessed the bulk of land as *zamindars* and intermediaries while the 'privileged' upper *Shudras* were the tillers of land as farmers. Sections inferior to them comprised the large pool of landless labourers and artisans working as support for the landed. Abolition of *zamindari* in spite of the changes introduced helped the perpetuation of upper caste dominance in rural setting as "large numbers of *zamindars* 'resumed' cultivation of their lands and became *raiyats*." This led to a situation that favoured the upper castes to emerge as "larger cultivators, often with holding greatly in excess of land ceilings imposed by the Congress government, holdings which they were able to retain through a combination of *benami* transfers, badly maintained land records and corruption. The upper backwards became the small cultivators, and the Harijans stayed where they were as landless labourers."[11] Such economic entrepreneurs from the upper castes that preferred to cultivate land themselves did so as gentle supervisors under the shelter of an umbrella or under a shade tree without soiling their hands. In situation where even this was not feasible the land was leased out to others on terms favourable to the owner.

The upper caste dominated primarily due to their superior pedigree. Ownership of land and employment in the state administration were the other resources enabling them to perpetuate their dominance. Among the various attributes of status the ritual standing of the individual tended to be most important. Upper caste persons commanded more respect than the middle range castes. Educated low caste person remained inferior to uneducated upper castes. Low income through employment in state bureaucracy earned more prestige than superior economic standing in business. The forces unleashed in the wake of freedom struggle were oblivious to the cumulative resource disadvantages of the inferiors in the social hierarchy.

The Bihar Pradesh Kisan Sabha sought to organise the peasants with moderate landholding against the aberrations in the *Zamindari* system. Some of its programmes suited peasants with identical background in the middle range castes. The Kisan Sabha was dominated by Bhumihars. Other upper castes were few and far between. Among the middle range castes only Koeris and Kurmis had 'occasional' presence in the organisation. The Bhumihar dominance simply neglected the strength of that group as the major element among the 'landed gentry' and 'adventurers' in the period. The leadership of the Sabha did not favour the middle range castes fit for inclusion within its fold. Then the Sabha had no concern for the problems of the small peasants and landless labourers thus ignoring the interests of large section of masses among the lower *shudras* and untouchables. One thing is, therefore, quite obvious that while the ritually superior and economically sound castes in the middle of the stratification asserted for proper space in the socio-economic and political structure and had their own organisations to further their interests those with slim margin of existence and placed lower to these castes in the caste hierarchy were in a deplorable state as none evinced interests in them.[12]

Upper caste dominated power structure remained oblivious to pressure for reform in agrarian structure. Effective steps to implement the proposed radical measures tended to be elusive. The indifference of the Congress party to its own 'no rent campaign' during the pre-Independence period and its legislative manipulations to thwart the state resolves for land reforms in the post-Independence phase illustrates the insincerity of the party in this regard. Bihar was "the first state to initiate agrarian reforms through the enactment of legislation to abolish the *zamindari* system and possibly the least successful of all in implementing that and other agrarian reforms. Nowhere in contemporary India is the gulf between articulated ideals with respect to agrarian reforms and solid accomplishments more conspicuous than in Bihar."[13]

Land reform measures were not sincerely implemented. Passage of the Land Ceiling Act was delayed as it affected the elites. The provisions for the abolition of *zamindari* contained loopholes that favoured the landlords in retaining the old possessions in new form. The delay in executing the *Zamindari* Abolition Act and the Land Ceiling Act was deliberate as it suited the interests of the ruling elite comprising the landlords. The state's bureaucratic apparatus had identical class interests as it mostly included the scions from the prosperous upper caste families opposed to changes in the *status quo*. In a state whose 83 per cent of the bureaucracy is constituted of upper castes implementation of legislations unfavourable to the traditionally embedded is difficult. In fact Bihar seems to be the only state where the employees of the government demonstrate against the implementation of the land reform measures.

Many years after independence little has been done in support of the share croppers and landless labourers. Tenants do not have security of tenures and their presence is never recorded. Prolonged attachment with particular plot of land is not allowed. Payment of exorbitant rent, uncertainty with regard to continuity of tenure, no hope for any claim on land ploughed as sharecropper continues. Under the arrangement the sharecropper is always the looser as he has to pay much in terms of labour and other necessary inputs and that too for little in terms of gains. He is worst affected if the weather turns unfavourable especially in cases the payment for the land ploughed is fixed. Such peasants "are left with little to subsist on and much less to invest." Landless labourers are in a worse situation as they are forced to survive on paltry payments received for their work. Wages fixed by the state were not available to them. Women are paid less than men. Coarse grains constitute part of the payments. The work is not available throughout the year. In the lean period they are rendered jobless. Plight of these poor in the situation of draught is deplorable. Situation like this compel the families to shift to towns nearer home forcing the women to indulge in sex trade. In fact the fate of the landless labourers especially the attached labourers "strike the most plaintive note in the agrarian order."[14]

On account of the tardy implementation of the land reform measures a substantial segment among such middle range castes as are landless labourers and sharecroppers still suffer from severe economic hardships. "The only significant consequence of the land reform programme was, therefore, to broaden the base of land control to include, apart from the upper castes, upper layers of the middle castes. The programme failed to provide succour to the genuine cultivators who laboured as insecure tenants-at-will. Further, as practically no headway was made in implementing the legislation on land ceilings the position of the land did not improve either."[15]

Economic prosperity is linked to caste status. In the predominantly rural economy of Bihar ownership of land remains the privilege of the select upper castes. It has been noted that landlords and rich peasants are to be found mostly among the upper castes. The study on rural economy in Bihar conducted under the auspices of the International Labour Office (ILO), Geneva has found 'a distinct overlap' between caste, class and landholding. It has noted landlords and big peasants in most of the cases are from the upper castes while the Scheduled Castes are essentially labourers. Castes listed as the most backward tend to have economic status similar to the Scheduled Castes as most of these castes are labourers working in others' farm. Similarly, most of the persons among the upper *shudras* especially among the Yadavas and Koeris are "poor-middle and middle peasants". The Kurmis, however, have been reported to be the most prosperous middle range caste as two thirds of them have been listed as "big peasants and landlords."[16] 95.7 per cent of the upper castes are reported to be landlord-*cum*-rich peasants. These castes have sparse presence among the middle level and lower peasantry. Among the upper middle castes more than one fourth are agricultural labourers. Such section from this social category that are characterised as middle or poor peasants have the strength of 36.75 per cent, while those described as landlord-*cum*-rich peasants account for 36.40 per cent of the population in this category. The most backward castes have overwhelming presence as agricultural labourers. 84.74 per cent of the families from this social category are agricultural wage earners. Among them next in strength are those who have been put in the category of middle peasants. 7.63 per cent households from this social category are to be found in this economic category. Those described as poor peasants have the strength of 3.39 per cent. The landlord-*cum*-rich peasants are few and far between in this social category. Thus as compared to the forward castes and the upper backward castes they have lower economic standing in Bihar. In spite of being put in the category of middle range castes, the most backward castes have little similarity with the castes described as upper backward castes. In fact their position is similar to the Scheduled Castes.[17] The middle range castes may be poor but the poorest are to be found among the Scheduled Castes. Some sections among the lower castes may have acquired prosperity replacing the upper castes in the structure of dominance where as most of the Scheduled Castes are still subservient in spite of the weakening of the traditional order. There is difference between poverty and insularity. Those who suffer economically may not be the victim of social deprivation. The socio-economic relationship between the middle range castes and the Scheduled Castes are not legitimised to the degree it used to be in the case of the upper castes. Such section in the lower castes find it difficult to enforce the pattern of domination traditionally endorsed in the favour of the upper castes. Attempts by the landowners with inferior social pedigree to legitimise surplus appropriation and newly acquired dominance are resisted even by 'the habitually subservient' at times resulting into eruption of violence.

The Naxalite movement was supported by the lower castes as it sought to pick the thread left in the past initiatives oriented to the upliftment of this section of society. Weakened traditional pattern of dominance and unacceptable terms in the new context of coercion push the economically vulnerable to favour the values and organisations championing violence as the most effective solution to the problems of exploitation. Such uprisings have occurred in the political periphery, where reach of the state is weak, social structure has failed to facilitate economic dynamism and the existing parties remain indifferent to the sad plight of the deprived thus providing political spaces to mobilise the peasantry. The sexual exploitation of women by the scions of the landlords turned out to be the immediate provocation for violent retaliation by the lower castes under the leadership of the Naxalites. In the villages dominated by the prosperous Bhumihars during the harvesting season such Scheduled Caste women as were willing to have sex with the landlord used to get some extra payments in addition to the wages they were entitled for their work. In one of such villages the orders of the landlords to engage the lower caste women for harvesting of crops in the night for their sexual exploitation turned to be the last straw leading to inauguration of an unprecedented phase of violent resistance against the intolerable designs of the upper caste landlords.

The movements led by the extremists in the left tends to be radical in nature and mark a unprecedented trend in peasant uprising in the countryside. These have the aim of raising the problems of the most exploited section of the society and had wide support of such people. Their Marxist leanings favour resort to violence. In the long history of peasant mobilisation problems of this section was never taken so seriously. The Bihar Pradesh Kisan Sangh took the lead in questioning some of the undue payments that land owning peasants were forced to make. Similarly, Triveni Sangh, an outfit of the select middle range castes, took some initiatives to raise the agrarian problems of the lower castes, however, it concerned itself exclusively with the agrarian problems of the elite among the upper *shudras* leaving the large section of poor and landless middle range castes helpless. The Communist parties intervened in situations seeking redressal to such problems. But, this too was not enough especially in the context of widening social inequality and rising frustration of the deprived sections against lack of institutionalised responses to provide effective solution to their problems. Started as sporadic eruptions Naxalism in course of time escalate in different parts of the state. Economic issues of land and wages and concern for the exploitation of lower caste women by the landowning upper castes have contributed to the emergence of such initiatives and have arranged widespread support for these outfits. Such groups not only have sustained long but also are fairly organised and have significant presence in the state. The top leaders are mainly ideologically wedded outsiders while the supporters are poor middle range castes and the Scheduled Castes. Some of them are organised as political parties and contest elections but at the grassroots trusted strategy to confrontations and assault has not been given up. Many people are reported to have been killed in the conflict between the two constituents of the village economy. Marxism succeeded in India at many places where percentage of landless households is fairly large and where most of its supporters are scheduled castes landless labourers. However, in Bihar there is a difference as members from other backward classes with similar class background as that of the Scheduled Castes are also members of the left extremist groups.

Out of 128 castes identified for state support and protection from among the middle range castes only three the Yadavas, Kurmis, and Koeris are important. These account for 18.5 per cent of the state population and 60 per cent of the total strength of the other backward classes. Most of them are medium sized landowners and are dominant throughout the state. Each of the three have their own areas of dominance. But, among them the Yadavas have overwhelming presence in all the districts. There are pockets where middle range castes with sound economic standing can be located. The Kurmis of Nalanda are well known in this regard. They are rich and educated. They have acquired land in the wake of *zamindari* abolition and have also purchased land from the Muslims migrating to Pakistan at low price. Commercial cropping has made them economically sound. They are reported to be ruthless in exploitation of labourers. Some of the infamous carnages against the *dalits* were committed by the Kurmis of the area. Politically also this place is important. The present Chief Minister of the state draws his political strength from this district. In the past also it has produced many leaders of eminence in the Congress Party. Such pockets are also to be found in the Patna district. Saharsa, "the Rome of the Yadavas" is the other island of prosperity so far as middle range castes are concerned. Here the Yadavs are the most prosperous and influential section of the population. Feudalism existed hand in hand to socialism in Saharsa. In the Kaimur district, there are Kurmis who are more prosperous than many of the upper caste families. Such affluence is also the characteristics of the Kurmis of Bhagalpur. The betel growers in Vaishali have few matches among the upper castes. However, there exists huge population among the middle range castes who are not so lucky. Most of the lower *shudras* are poor. Socially and economically they are more close to the Scheduled Castes than the upper *shudras* who are not only economically sound but also occupy superior social status and have wider representation in the institutions of power. While the upper *shudras* have separate areas of concentration, the lower *shudras* are scattered throughout the state in small numbers and are tied to their patrons in the upper castes as clients under the *jajmani* relationship.

The educational policy of the colonial regime favoured its spread among the upper stratum of the society. The low and poor tended to be excluded on account of its sectarian scope. The initial takers to the new education also appeared parochial as they used it to serve the interests of their own caste. Education, therefore, had limited spread in the early years of the colonial administration. It was more confined among the Kayasthas who had a tradition of working as writers and record keepers. They were employed "to draft documents of assignment of lands and villages, and of gradually increasing items of revenue given in grants." Its caste leaders took great interest in wider spread of education in the community with the huge fund arranged through donations. In subsequent years other upper castes mainly on account of declining fortunes in the rural areas got attracted towards the new education as it was necessary to find place in the prevalent opportunity structure. In this pursuit the support of the caste associations especially of the prosperous members turned crucial. This was most evident in the case of Bhumihars whose caste associations not only resolved to have institutions of learning for the spread of education in the caste but in fact made its wealthy members to turn the resolution into a reality. The first degree college of the north Bihar was established in Muzaffarpur and was named as Bhumihar Brahman College with the financial support of Langat Singh who was a railway contractor from this caste. Special scholarship and other suitable financial incentives were arranged with the help of some other landed and prosperous caste members. Such support was not available for the lower castes making them unsuitable in the emerging contexts. The elites of other upper castes also made the people of their castes realise the need for acquisition of new education. They established the first institutions of higher education in Bihar to enable the members of their caste to equip themselves effectively for suitable placements in the administrative structure evolved by the alien rulers. Centres thus started to cater to the needs of the sectarian interests served to strengthen the hold of caste in education and administration. This led to inauguration of a phase where different castes of Bihar especially the upper castes revealed for the first time their incline to ensure the placement of their own caste men in state services. While the Kayasthas provided the lead, other upper castes followed them. It has, however, to be noted that such castes who were not educated lagged far behind the upper castes in education and placement in the new opportunity structure. Thus at a time when the colleges in Bihar had an overwhelming presence of the upper castes, the lower castes had insignificant representation. The strength of the students of these castes was as meagre as 0.85 per cent of the total enrolment.[18] Such sections were not even literate to the level the upper castes were. Among the lower castes the Kalwars were the most literate. "Other castes in the intermediate layers do not seem to differ from each other in any significant manner."[19] The lead established by the upper castes in the field of education enabled them to reinforce their traditionally ordained superiority with the help of this newly acquired attribute of social status. The lower castes remained inferior to them. Thus, the colonial education tended to be selective so far as the spread of education among different social segments are concerned. It favoured the upper castes more than the *shudras* and untouchables. Uneven spread of education in turn implied lopsided distribution of privileges as education is an important resource to facilitate placements in politics, business and bureaucracy.

The lower castes' concern for education increased in the years after Independence. It, however, tended to be slow and remained confined to the dominant middle range castes with sound economic standing. The upper castes meanwhile with the support of their caste leaders established schools and colleges in large numbers in different parts of Bihar providing in this way wider spread of education. Teachers and office staff in such institutions used to be mostly from the caste that 'owned' the institution. On being taken over by the state such 'academicians' who in many cases were not fit to be a clerk became entitled to impressive salaries and privileges from the state coffer. This sponsored dominance of 'rejects' in the 'temples of learning' ultimately caused irreparable damage to the quality of education in the state. In this crime every caste excepting those included as the Scheduled Castes was involved. One document detailing the history of the Kurmis maintains that this caste has till 1986 established 33 colleges in different districts of Bihar.[20] This number must have increased now. So far as the Yadavas are concerned they have large number of colleges named after Ram Lakhan Singh Yadava, once the most important leader of the Yadavas. These notwithstanding the upper castes were more successful than their counterparts in the middle range castes as the so called education mafia. They played crucial role in setting private medical colleges and getting them affiliated to the universities of the state and in arranging for them required recognition through their connections in the Medical Council and the State Government. With the proliferation of public schools affiliated to federal control boards the upper castes have further tightened their control on education by establishing centres for 'quality education' in Bihar.

Such has been the control of the upper castes in educational set-up of Bihar that each of its universities had a distinct caste character. Thus, the Magadh University used to be called the Chittorgarh of Bihar on account of the large scale presence of Rajput teachers, the L.N. Mithila University was dominated by Brahmins that too from Mithila. In the Bihar University Bhumihars were the most powerful. The united front of other upper castes that existed there under the leadership of Rajputs failed to disturb the equilibrium favouring the dominance of the

Bhumihars. The Patna University as well as the Bhagalpur University had the presence of separate permutations of upper castes. While in Patna the Kayastha had impressive presence it was not the case in the Bhagalpur University that tended to be dominated by Bhumihars and Brahmins. Such features affected the caste composition of the teachers in different departments.

In spite of the fact that now there is no denial of entry to the lower castes in the institutions of learning and in spite of the fact that such sections can now afford education to their children, it is found that the middle range castes lag behind the upper castes in acquisition of education. In a study conducted by the International Labour Organisation some time back in rural Bihar, it was found that the incidence of education is high among the upper castes while the middle range castes seem to lag behind them. Among the middle range castes, Kurmis and Koeris have been found more inclined to send their children to schools than the Yadavas. Similar is the orientation of the extremely backward castes. So far as the Kurmis are concerned, they are closely emulating the upper castes especially in their areas of concentration not only in school enrolments but also in keeping the women of their households away from participation as labour force. The Koeris and Yadavas also do not favour the presence of the women from their castes as field workers.[21]

Heterogeneity characterising the category often splits OBC to different options in politics. Thus the umbrella shelter of the Congress under the one party dominance system was available mainly to the rich and sophisticated from the ritually superiors among the middle range castes. Such leaders tended to have surrogate status in the party dominated by the upper castes. Parties in the opposition in spite of the support of the middle range castes also had the similar leadership structure. Strong presence in centres of power and political consciousness enabled them to assert for reserved accommodation in the state structures for administration. Caste polarisation that ensued the implementation of the recommendations of the Mandal Commission seems to have narrowed the inner differentiation within the category of the other backward classes favouring support to the parties and leadership wedded to the interests of the middle range castes.

The other backward classes in Bihar, thus failed to compensate for inherited inferiority in their status through the acquisition of modern attributes of status to the extent that they could claim parity of status with the traditionally superior. While they suffered the lag, the upper caste enhanced the lead available to them. Within the middle range castes benefits of development has skewed distribution. The select few among this section have been more successful than their not so lucky brethren. The existence of resources does not automatically leads to their even distribution among different segments of society.

REFERENCES

1. Susan Bayly, (2005), *Caste, Society and Politics in India,* Cambridge University Press, Cambridge, p. 286.
2. L.I. Rudoph and Susanne Rudolph, (1987), *In Pursuit of Lakshmi,* Orient Longman, Bombay.
3. Meenakshi Jain, (1997), "Backward Classes and Social Changes in UP and Bihar" in *Caste—Its Twentieth Century Avtar,* (ed.) by M.N. Srinivas, Penguin Books India P Ltd., New Delhi.
4. Marcus Franda, *Small is Politics,* Wiley Eastern Ltd., New Delhi, p. 233.
5. G. Thimmiah, (1993), *Power Politics and Social Justice,* Sage Publications, New Delhi, p. 36.
6. L.I. Rudolph and Rudolph Susanne, (1984), "Determinants and Varieties of Agrarian Mobilisation" in *Agrarian Productivity in South Asia* (ed.) Meghnad Desai *et al.,* Oxford University Press, New Delhi, p. 323.
7. R.K. Hebsur, (1980), *Bihar: Fragmented and Telescoped Backward Classes Movement,* Report of the Mandal Commission, Government of India, p. 160.
8. *See* Appendix 2.
9. Kalyan Mukherjee and Rajendra Singh Yadav, (1980), *Bhojpur: Naxalism in the Plains of Bihar,* Radhakrishna Prakashan, New Delhi, p. 35.
10. Atul Kohli, (1992), *Democracy and Discontent,* Cambridge University Press, Cambridge.
11. Harry W. Blair (1980), "Rising Kulaks and Backward classes in Bihar", *Economic and Political Weekly,* Vol. 15, No. 21.
12. Kalyan Mukherjee and Rajendra Singh Yadav, *op. cit.*
13. F. Tomasson Jannuzi, (1989). *India in Transition,* Orient and Longman, Bombay.
14. Kalyan Mukkherjee and Rajendra Singh Yadav, *op. cit.*
15. Anand Chakravarti, (2001), "Caste and Agrarian Class: A view from Bihar," *Economic and Political Weekly,* Vol. 36, No. 7.

16. P.H. Prasad and G.B. Rodgers, *Caste, Class and Landholding in the Analysis of the Rural Economy*, (mimo) International Labour Office, Geneva n.d.
17. Pradhan H. Prasad, (1989), *Poor Peasant Movement in Central Bihar (typescript).*
18. Hetukar Jha, (1985), *Colonial Context of Higher Education in India*, Usha Publications, New Delhi, p. 67.
19. Ibid., p. 69.
20. Ram Krishna Mehta, (1986), *Rohan Aya Ghar Rohi Nahi*, Janjagran Prakashan Samaj, Patna.
21. Pradhan H. Prasad, G.B. Roggers, *op. cit.*, p. 47.

3

Quest for Mobility

An Analysis of Other Backward Classes Movement in the Historical Perspective

Opposition to the dominance of the Brahmins as institutionalised in social movements of the western and the southern India, called non-Brahmanism, constituted the 'first point' at which members of peasant castes, and other traditionally non-literate castes organised themselves to advance their own claims at 'supra-local level'.[1] It was "strongest in peninsular India where only one caste, the Brahmins enjoyed preponderance in higher education, the profession and government employment" and "where a wide social and cultural gulf obtained between the Brahmins and others."[2] It manifested an urge for social equality in a context where traditional as well as modern attributes of status coalesced in favour of a single caste. Such stirrings marked the inauguration of a phase where the traditionally privileged encountered organised assault to the privileges available to them. The protests and assertions reflected opposition to the value system which legitimised the super ordination of the Brahmins. Social transformation that followed could be possible with the support of networks comprising social identities seeking redemption from traditionally ordained disabilities. Caste associations of lower status groups were instrumental in preparing them for effective articulation of their unease.

Jyoti Rao Govind Rao Phule was the first significant leader from the middle range castes to articulate effectively the *shudra's* unease over the inequality and exploitation embodied in the caste system. Phule experienced deep shock at being treated as social inferiors by Brahmins who accepted him as intellectual equal.[3] His transformation as crusader for dignity to the deprived and excluded was possible on this account. Personal issues compelled him to take the fight on a wider arena. Phule's ideology for social change represented a constellation of many ideas and influences. He seems to have been influenced by liberalism of the West, egalitarianism in the Christianity and indigenous writings on the inequalities in the caste system.[4] Phule preferred equality to political freedom. His was the first voice of protest against the inequality in the caste system. Under his leadership the Indian society witnessed the inauguration of a movement that emphasised the importance of equality and rationality in determining the interpersonal relationships among the different sections. Phule did not approve the 'intermediacy' of priesthood as he considered "individual conscience and reason (to be) his best guide to spiritual progress."[5] His crusade against iniquitous arrangement enshrined in the Hindu social order and legitimised in tradition probably would not have acquired efficacy had he been from a community who had not suffered this humiliation. The stirring sought to "question and negate the assumption and attribution of inequality of status based on birth."[6] The Satya Sodhak Samaj that he founded had the objective of exposing the Brahmins for their use of the caste system for the purpose of exploitating the middle and lower status castes. The prevalent Hindu social order made the Brahmins indispensable for securing religious merit for an individual. In the Hindu rituals the presence of Brahmin was necessary as it conferred prestige to the individual performing the ritual. The Samaj encouraged the non-Brahmin population to "substitute their own celebrants for Brahmin religious ceremonies and *rites de passage* and to guard against exploitation by Brahmin officials."[7] The Satya Sodhak Samaj in spite of being inclusive derived its strength from the caste of its leader. It, however, did not seek to serve the interest of this single caste. The effectiveness of the crusade initiated by Phule was evident in quiet and unprecedented shift in the locus of power as the dominant lower castes spearheading the movement found significant space in the Congress Party of the state. The key role in such activities was played by Shahu Chhatrapati who in addition to arranging wider space for these sections in the occupational structure emphasised their elevation in the Hindu social order. In its subsequent phase the movement was successful in ensuring large-scale accommodation of the lower castes in the state services. It drew inspirations from the leadership of Chhatrapati Sahu of Kolhapur who as its patron played an effective role in spread of education among these castes. Support to his initiatives found support among the Marathas as he successfully utilised their Kshatriya pride in his fight against the dominant Brahmins. Thus the strategies adopted in the subsequent phase were different from those in the initial phase as the movement during this phase reflected fondness for the symbols of superior pedigree. This was evident from the importance accorded to thread-investiture ceremonies that had the intention of conferring Kshatriya status to Marathas and similar cther castes. The Satya Sodhak Samaj was also favourably inclined to the initiatives of Sahu as he was poised to their uplift.

The non-Brahmin movement considered to be the 'first of the backward class movements' in Tamil Nadu[8] was launched by a narrow elite 'from families with generations of involvement in the government services and the professions behind them"[9] and comprised *rajas, zamindars,* industrialists, lawyers, and doctors.[10] Subsequently, it acquired a wide support leading to far reaching socio-political changes. It had the objective of securing recruitment in the state services for such communities which were traditionally inferior to the Brahmins in the caste hierarchy and were unable to compete with them in securing placement in the state services. It was felt that the real issue was the dominance of a caste that on account of its knowledge of the language of colonial administration "absorbed all the government appointments great and small, high and low" leading to exclusion of even the 'men of capacity enlightenment and culture' from other castes in state services. Such situation it was maintained warranted weakening of the hold of caste through wider spread of education and socio-economic and political development and did not require practices that had the intentions to perpetuate the *status quo*. In order to make themselves equal to the entrenched elite groups the leaders of the movement not only took resort to construction of myths pertaining to their origin, but also pressed the government for special treatment in state services and initiated a crusade for separating the state from Indian national state. With the passage of time such themes acquired more and more intensity leading to institutionalisation of the movements with the formation of a non-

Brahmin organisation under the leadership of E.V. Ramaswamy Naicker who established the 'Self-Respect Movement'. It concentrated on the poorer classes and low castes, both poor cultivators and untouchables as well as women and young people. It ridiculed Brahmanical literature rituals and pretensions.[11] He took it out of its concern for proportional representation. Naicker launched an attack "on the whole Brahmanic ideology of privilege scriptural in general, and religion either as general ethos or as theological doctrine."[12] The aim was to destroy the beliefs and practices legitimised under the caste system. The campaign sustained long as it acquired wide receptivity. Initiated as social reform movement oriented to provide redemption from ritual dominance and cultural pre-eminence of the Brahmins, it subsequently used its strength to arrange favours for the backward classes from the colonial administration and princely rulers as quid *pro quo* to their opposition to the nationalist movement. These initiatives contributed significantly towards development of a 'bargaining culture' and made it possible for the middle range castes to avail provisions for special dispensation. The non-Brahmin movement in Tamil Nadu seems to have spent itself, having achieved its principal objectives. The unity of the non-Brahmins has been loosened after they gained ascendancy.[13]

The non-Brahmin movement in Karnataka owes its initiation to the development in the neighbouring Madras Presidency and was started to articulate the inadequate representation of non-Brahmins in the services of the Mysore Princely State dominated by the Brahmins. The privileged location of the Brahmins in the administrative structure of the state had facilitated large scale induction of their caste men in the services of the state. In the process the non–Brahmins were excluded at times in violation of the directives favouring their recruitment. Such manipulations aimed at the exclusion of the non-Brahmins constituted the main concern of the non-Brahmin movement that was soon launched. Social networking of individual castes lent strength to the stirrings that followed. Each of the two dominant castes comprising the core activated para-communities to mobilise their caste men against this injustice. The urge to have share in the administrative power system ceased to be nebulous as the individual initiatives of each of these castes acquired institutionalisation with the formation of an organisation named Praja Mitra Mandali. Under its auspices the heterogeneous non-Brahmin groups were united to make claims for adequate representation in the state administration. In this struggle the Vokkaligas and the Lingayats who led the movement had the complementary support of the Muslims, Christians and other communities nurturing identical aspirations. The Scheduled Castes in spite of their numerical strength failed to have an independent course that could specifically suit their interests and supported the dominant groups in their pursuit for equality. In spite of being confined to places dominated by the Brahmins it produced desired results as provisions for reservation to the non-Brahmins in the state services turned out to be a reality. The unity thus arrived, however, did not sustain long as the outfits wedded to the upliftment of the lower castes merged with the Congress Party to work under the leadership of the Brahmins who dominated the party. Its decline is also attributed to the fact that it had limited intentions and had no radical socio-economic programme that could lend it prolonged durability. Communally sensitive section among the non-Brahmin castes subsequently formed a separate party and named it Praja Paksha. Once the mistake was realised the two outfits representing the interests of the non-Brahmin castes merged to form Praja Samyukta Mandali. Manifestation of inner contradictions notwithstanding this constellation of mobility-oriented section constituted the nucleus for the different backward classes movement in Karnataka. The movement contributed significantly in strengthening the position of the Lingayats and Vokalligas who subsequently emerged as the lead caste in the state politics. The dominance of these two castes was in course of time weakened with the emergence of the smaller backward castes. The most important step that the Karnataka Government took to weaken the landed interests of the Brahmins in the post-Independence India related to conferring of ownership rights to the tillers of the Imam land that were owned by the Brahmins.

The Telugu-speaking coastal districts in the Madras Presidency that tended to be "the strongholds of Brahmin orthodoxy" were important centres of the activities challenging the dominance of the Brahmins. The term 'Brahmanethavodyamamu' implied the welter of movements operative in Telugu areas organised by people who were not

Brahmins.[14] In these areas the lead to oppose the dominance of Brahmin was taken by the land owning and politically conscious. Kammas, Reddis, and Velamas. These castes occupied low ritual status and had sparse presence in bureaucracy on account of the dominance of the Brahmins. The leaders in the movement questioned the legitimisation of the superiority-inferiority scale describing it a manipulation of the Brahmins to arrogate ritual exclusiveness for themselves. Then, in order to ensure reasonable presence of the non-Brahmins in the bureaucracy demand for 'non-Brahminisation of services' was made. It was argued that since the non-Brahmins paid more revenue than the Brahmins and had numerical superiority they deserve adequate representation in the services of the empire to whom they were loyal. The movement had two sides. On the one hand there were leaders who made concerted efforts to prepare the masses against Brahmanism as the way of life. There were others who held them guilty for distorting the original religious order to serve their own interests. Such leaders considered them sinful for committing exclusivism and depriving other *varnas* from the benefits due to them. The movement in spite of being opposed to Brahmins did not favour the destruction of the order that perpetuated social inequality as the different castes sought superior location in the status-structure traditionally ordained. In order to compete with the Brahmins in the services the caste associations of individual dominant non-Brahmin castes put emphasis on spread of education. Hostels to accommodate students from these castes were started and financial support was provided. It was realised that the non-Brahmins had to first equip themselves in order to seek upward mobility. Competing claims of superiority and caste-specific self-help groups (SHGs), however, did not favour emergence of integrated initiatives for corporate status striving among these castes. The unity that existed failed to sustain long as the weak but numerically dominant non-Brahmins were denied reservation in jobs in proportion to their numerical strength. With the passage of time it became a spent force. It thus appears that the non-Brahmin movement in this part of the country was committed to limited gains and once it succeeded in attaining the goal it turned out to be irrelevant.

In conclusion it can be said that the non-Brahmin movement was inspired by values disfavouring privileges and discrimination legitimised by the traditional stratification system and was wedded to removal of the Brahmanical culture and dominance. It was initiated in the western and southern states of the country characterised by extremely orthodox and rigid social order. In these places the Brahmins kept themselves insulated from the rest of the population as their ritual status conferred to them unquestioned supremacy. Economically as owners of land they wielded considerable influence over the landless. They were also the first to respond to westernisation. Since they were traditionally a literate caste they encountered least problem in learning the language of the new rulers. This made them most competent to find placement in the colonial administration. This added a new feather to their cap as the traditional as well as modern attributes of status congrued in their favour contributing to the escalation of the pre-existing gap between them and the rest of the population.

It is also evident that these movements in order to be successful required leaders from among the section having experience of deprivation. These had to be personally a deviant oriented to promotion of a social order that had to be different from the old and resilient. It is also clear that initial support to such stirrings came from such lower castes which had significant number of educated persons and had presence in the urban areas. Experiences of disabilities turned out to be better facilitator for the outbreak of protest than its perception as a construct. The contradiction between the dominant status and salient status of the leaders seems to have prompted them to initiate stirrings to seek legitmation to the status that suited their aspiration.[15] Perceived feasibility to usher in dispersal in the context of cumulative inequality tended to be facilitative for the launch of stirrings for change.

Non-Brahmanism it seems to have subsequently emerged as a political force uniting a mixed array of service, commercial groups and superior clean-caste/*sat-sudra* peasant groups.[16] The context of one caste dominance was certainly the main reason for the emergence of new forces opposed to such dominance. However, the social unease thus articulated acquired strength through the indirect support of the colonial administration which promoted it "as a counter-weight to the voice of the 'Brahman subversives' in the newly enhanced municipal and provincial councils." The term 'non-Brahmanism' thus represented a political coalition of the diverse social entities temporarily in alliance for the attainment of certain immediate interests with the support of the colonial administration. Sense of identity and unity of purpose manifested in the wake of the non-Brahmanical movement produced ripple effects. The movement has been so successful in south that the Brahmins are today deprived of their traditional superiority and had left their own homeland to settle elsewhere in India. Those who were unable to find out such options are to be found in towns of their own states after rupturing their rural connections. Federative strength seems to have produced impressive dividends as long as the inherent diversities were kept under check. The southern states, where such initiatives initially articulated, were in the course of time unable to sustain the spirit of anti-Brahmanism and extend the movement to its "logical end of sustaining and expanding its base for eradicating the caste system."[17]

The non-Brahmin movements have been interpreted in different ways by different scholars. These have been in the first place seen as caste movements meant to provide "new or amplified meanings to caste linkages and thus to caste itself". Ideological components crucial in these led other analysts to characterised them as stirrings seeking redemption from the alien intrusion upon an indigenous culture. Such analysts saw in these attempts an urge to instill in the culturally dominated social groups the need to aggregate themselves for collective assertion through acquisition of an identity that places them at par with the dominant. Since the movements succeeded in facilitating the rise of the deprived sections, these were also viewed as campaigns to capture power in which non-Brahminism was used for support recruitment. The leaders in such movements in some other works have been considered as the new elites that ultimately turned replacements to the elites uprooted. Those interested in the analysis of the class composition of the leadership and support structure in these collective strivings have indicated that the movements reflected the aspirations of the sections that acquired prosperity on account of the programmes for development initiated by the colonial administration.[18]

Bihar did not witness formalised opposition to the dominance of cluster of castes occupying the apex of stratification in the manner the Brahmins were opposed in the southern part of the country. Some attempts are reported to have been made much after the successful replacement of the Brahmins in the south that seems to articulate the desire of the lower castes to climb up in the caste hierarchy. In order to fulfil such mobility aspirations steps were taken by the well off middle range castes to internalise *samskritika* values. This process is also dubbed as 'peasant *Vaishnavism'* when "the small holders of Ram- and Krishna-loving Kurmi and Ahir-Yadav origin donned the sacred thread as self-styled Kshatriyas." The organisations that were formed to ensure the elevation of the lower castes in the status-structure came quite late and had elitist orientations and limited spread. The strategies pursued did not question the privileges and domination of specific castes superior in the hierarchy. Emphasis was on seeking mobility within the parameters of Brahmanic ideology. The initial years of the twentieth century were witness to proliferation of caste associations formed by the different middle range castes. These aimed at elevation of their status in the traditional stratification. Individual castes had their own leaders and their own individual support structure. They however, had common purpose and identical strategies. Each caste claimed descendance to different Hindu Gods or to some legendary figures from upper castes. Internalisation of upper caste values and behavioural pattern used to be the next step. Often old names of the castes were discarded to obtain new names indicating superior location in the caste system. In order to appear like the castes with whom they claim parity suitable changes in diet were suggested to be made. Certain items of food and drink that were not taken by the upper castes were sought to be avoided. Changes in the institution of marriage were recommended to avoid child marriage and to prohibit widow remarriage. Some of the middle range castes took initiatives to question the monopoly of the upper castes over Hindu rituals and privileges. One important step in this regard was their decision to don sacred thread that used to be a symbol of *Savarna* caste. It was not an attempt to imitate, instead it reflected a determination to claim equality with the sections located at the apex. It represented a process of aggression by which they challenged the monopoly of the upper castes in the use of religious goods and services of Brahmanical Hinduism from which they have been kept out for centuries.

The Yadavas constitute the most important caste among the middle range castes of Bihar. They are described as the most distinguishable *Aryans* with highest virtues attracting God "to be incarnated amongst them, to play with them, to sing the sweet melody of the *Bhagavad Gita* in order to bring peace and prosperity in the world. Without the help of the Yadava, Shri Krishna could not have done anything."[19] The first caste association of the Yadavas of Bihar known as Gop Jatiya Maha Sabha was founded in 1912. It had the intention of raising the location of the Yadavas in the traditional stratification system. The organisation claimed that Yadavas were Kshatriyas and were entitled to wear sacred threads. In the subsequent years other issues mostly related to their economic interests captured the attention of such organised caste outfits. In such interactions with the caste men the importance of education was stressed, equality with the superiors in the hierarchy was sought to be acquired, and exploitation especially as forced labourer was considered to be intolerable. The caste associations of the Yadavas while oriented to upward mobility in the caste hierarchy took up issues pertaining to economic exploitation of the members of the caste. In the conferences resolutions were passed expressing opposition to forced unpaid labour. The Yadavas sought fair prices for the milk and milk product as certain sections among the landlords and Government servant forced them to sale these at lower prices. Use of common land was not allowed causing lot of hardships to them. These issues also received the attention of the Yadava caste association. The Gop Jatiya Maha Sabha in the year 1923 made demands for representation of Yadavas in different local bodies. Thus the strategies adopted by the caste association for elevation of the status of caste men had secular as well as traditional components.[20] While the prevalent socio-economic suoordination appeared to be unacceptable, no attempt was made to question the ingrained value system that legitimised social inequality. The Yadavas 'tried to upgrade themselves' within the traditional stratification system by internalising the symbols of superiority endorsed by the Brahmins and demanded an end to their exploitation. Their organised protests against economic exploitation and ritual inferiority were not liked by the upper castes. They had to encounter violent protests from the upper castes at many places. Non-availability of milk at privileged rate irked the Muslim landlords of Bihar Sharif who in turn implicated the Yadavas in false cases. The upper castes opposed the use of sacred thread by persons of the lower castes. Crowds comprising such angry upper castes seeking removal of sacred threads from their person had to encounter violent resistance. The Yadavas did not succumb to such manipulations. In response to the retaliation of the landlords that followed they organised meetings and held demonstrations in many parts of the state. They turned violent to resist suppression. The colonial officials in their reports on the clashes maintained that by wearing sacred thread the lower castes especially the Yadavas not only sought upper caste status but also claimed impunity from rendering menial and other services for the upper castes. Thus the riots triggered in the wake of the assertion of the upward mobile middle range castes reflected their unease over the socio-economic dominance of the forces of *status quo*. The Yadavas of Bihar represented a significant section of the All India Yadav Maha Sabha formed after the merger of regional associations. This federation urged the caste men to turn vegetarian and avoid alcohol. In its recommendations opening in the modern occupations was considered important deserving attention of the Yadavas. It urged the members to put pressure on the Government for special treatment to Yadavas in military.

The Kurmis constituted 3.6 per cent of the population of the undivided Bihar. Agriculture is their main occupation. Considered economically prosperous and politically dominant middle range castes like the Yadavas they claim a Kshaṭriya status for themselves. Stories on their origin emphasising "an ancient past of Kshatriya distinction that had long since deteriorated into present-day *Shudra* dishonour" are quite old.[21] Kurmis of Bihar consider themselves to be the descendants of Lav, one of the two sons of lord Rama, while the Koeris claim descendance from Kush, the second son of the lord. Perhaps, this is the reason the two castes are together in the politics of Bihar. In fact earlier also attempts for federating the two castes were made when suggestions for creating Raghav Samaj was mooted. It did not succeeded then on account of the rivalries between the leaders of the two castes.[22]

The Kurmi caste association was founded in Awadh in the year 1894. The spur was the colonial Government decision to declare them as a criminal caste preventing their recruitment into Police and Army. The caste association aimed at integration of cognate sub-castes to spread caste consciousness. The Mahtos

Kurmis in Chotanagpur considered as Hinduised tribals and the Dhanuks of the North Bihar linked up with the Awadhia Kurmis as parts of All-India Kurmi Mahasabha. The Kurmis not only claimed the status of the Kshatriyas but also rechristened their association as the All India Kurmi Kshatriya Mahasabha with its registered office in Patna. Sanskritik values acquired priority concern in its programmes. The Mahasabha, however, had some other concerns as it pleaded for reservations in employment available to the weaker section of the society. It has to be noted here that the association in its initial phase had pressed the Government for according the Kurmis the Kshatriya status. The Arya Samaj helped them to internalise sanskritik values and in claiming descent from the God Indra to claim Kshatriya status.[23] The caste associations of the Kurmis derived their leadership from among the educated and economically prosperous section of the community especially in the initial phase. Subsequently, persons distinguished in professions and politics took the command.[24] Kurmis claim to divine origin is also indicated as they take pride in being the descendants of the tortoise that according to the Hindu Mythology was the incarnation of Lord Vishnu and protected the earth from water to create the organic milieu. Caste historians relate Kurmis to Lord Rama and to rain God Indra. The Sabha sought to include in its fold some cultivating castes from other states of the country whom it considered to be Kurmis. In its consideration the Patidars of Gujarat, the Kapus of Andhra Pradesh, the Vokkaligas of Karnataka the Reddys and Naidus of the Madras presidency, and the Marathas of Maharashtra were Kurmis.[25]

The Koeris claim decadence to Kush one of the sons of Lord Rama and call themselves Kushwaha. Lord Buddha and King Chandragupta are mentioned as their ancestors. Most of them claim to be Kshatriya while there are Koeris who claim the status of Brahmins. Koeris have their own caste associations. Their first caste association was known as Koeri Hitkari Sabha which later assumed the name of Kushwaha Kshatriya Mahasabha. In spite of the fact that the organisation had within its fold Koeris from Uttar Pradesh most of its sessions were held in Bihar. The association sought to unite different branches of the caste with the aim to ensure its socio-economic and cultural development. Political leaders from this caste in spite of their ideological differences and being affiliated to different political parties supported its activities.

Claims of superior lineage, however, were not helpful to the middle range castes in lifting themselves to an elevated location in the caste hierarchy. Constraints of inherited inferiority did not favour them in appropriation of 'traditional symbols of honour' to which they were not entitled. Sanskritisation soon lost its sheen as it could not arrange for them social privileges available to the superiors in the caste hierarchy. Symbolic satisfaction could not be a substitute for socio-economic equality.

It is maintained that the caste associations in spite of their failure to arrange elevated location to the middle range castes played a crucial role in securing some benefits for the castes that these represented. These enabled them to get better returns for their products. Spread of education among the lower castes was facilitated through the efforts made by the associations. Schools were established to cater to the rising aspirations of the youth. Scholarship provisions were made for the deserving caste men. Since many students came to these schools from far off places hostel accommodations were arranged. Sanskritisation was considered a panacea to get redemption from the fetters of exploitation. It was perhaps the only resort open to them in absence of initiatives wedded to restructuring of the economic order. The Kisan movement led by Swami Sahjanand failed to inspire the confidence of peasants from the lower castes whereas the caste associations supported such initiatives. It may, however, be mentioned that social fragmentation among the lower *shudras* constrained their emergence as a cohesive unit.

Such initiatives, however, failed to produce opposition to Brahmins in the way it was the case in the states where the supremacy of the Brahmins were aggressively questioned. The mobilisation of the Yadavas through the caste associations, however, seem to have narrowed the distance among the different endogamous sub-castes comprising this ethnic category. Such social fusion fostered caste solidarity could be used for socio-economic betterment and for political gains. However, "a more ambitious ethnicisation process" tended to be elusive as other castes with identical claims for ritual superiority did not favour fusion to form caste federation. In the initial phase concern for individual caste mobility fostered the context of insularity among such social categories. Sanskritisation does not favour federation of castes placed differentially in the caste hierarchy. Diverse interests find better redressal in the loose and frequently changing composition of informal caste federation wedded to serve political interests. The ethnic identity thus prepared for assertion was "embedded in the sanskritisation logic,"[26] and was in sharp contrast to the Bahujan or a Dravidian identity of the lower castes in the south who claimed to be the original inhabitants of the country.

The first successful attempts for the unity of the important middle range caste seems to have been made in Bihar when the Yadavas, the Kurmis and the Koeris decided to organise themselves in the local district board elections of 1930. This was followed by the coming up of a federation of these castes named as the Triveni Sangh. The Sangh was committed to ensure solidarity among people of different sections from three castes so as to enable them to participate unitedly in democratic politics and to make it possible for them to effectively resist the oppressive upper castes from exploiting them. The Sangh was named Triveni after the confluence of three sacred rivers in Allahabad. The leadership of the Sangh was drawn from educated professionals among the Kurmis and Yadavas. With the passage of time such persons who had personal experience of caste discrimination and had turned bitter critics of upper caste dominance took the command of the Sangh. This coming together of the three middle range castes with common cultural and ethnic background heralded the inauguration of a process of empowerment of forces located in the middle of the stratification system determined to challenge the political strength of the numerically weak but ritually superior social categories. Subsequently, it became more inclusive at least apparently as its ideologue presented it as an organisation wedded to safeguard the interests of peasants, landless labourers and small traders. Its merger with the backward class organisations led to inclusion in its fold other lower castes such as *Bania, Teli, Kumhar, Kanhar* etc. *Shudra* uprising that was triggered in the wake of the integration of the lower castes posed a challenge to the upper caste dominated Congress party. Its survival in spite of attempts for its dismemberment firstly through a proposal for its merger in the Congress party and then through an attempt to take the other lower castes in the Depressed Classes League was not to the liking of the leadership in the Congress party. An important leader of the party described its existence as manifestation of undesirable casteism and an evil that accompanied recently endowment of power to the enslaved masses. One of the prominent leaders of the Sangh is reported to have disclosed that even Gandhi did not like its activities. Upper caste people did not endorse the Sangh decisions to contest elections. Pre-election campaigns in 1937 turned violent resulted in killings and assaults on the persons of these castes. Supporters of the Sangh were identified after the elections and were assaulted. The surprise success of the Sangh's candidates even in limited numbers in the Shahabad District Board election in 1938 reflected the growing strength of the middle range castes in politics. In the 1937 elections it succeeded in some limited areas. The Sangh favoured reservation for the middle range castes and made it an important issue in the 1946 elections demanding 40 per cent reservation for the members of such communities. This *Shudra* uprising under this independent organisation was a challenge to the upper caste dominated Congress party.

The Sangh, however, remained operative among the three upper *shudra* castes and its leadership remained confined to wealthy land owning professionals from these castes. Its programmes reflected "a caste response to an essentially class problem". Perceived as an 'Ahir-Koeri-Kurmi Syndicate' it failed to attract the many other lower castes and was, therefore, unable to make substantive dents in the support structure of the Congress party. Its potential as powerful interests group could not escape the attention of the leaders in the Congress. The party became more accommodative to include a few important leaders from the Sangh as the office bearers in the organisation. In the elections that ensued subsequently the leaders of the Sangh contested as candidates of the Congress party. Context witnessing cleavages between the upper castes and the middle range castes lost its sharpness as Sangh lost its individual existence in the wake of its merger in the Congress sponsored Backward Classes Federation in 1948.

It did not exist long mainly on account of the unwillingness of castes to stay as equals and partly on account of the manipulations of the upper castes to split the emerging leadership in the name of serving the larger interests of the national politics. The superior-inferior syndrome characterising the instincts of graded inequality embedded in the caste system appeared inimical to the unity of differentially placed lower castes. While claiming equality of status with the upper castes certain sections appeared unprepared to treat castes below them to be equal to them. Thus, the Yadavas projected themselves not only as superiors to the other constituents in the middle of the traditional stratification system but also considered themselves to be the 'natural leaders' of the backward classes.[27] Stories from the Vedic past were cited to endorse their claims. Lure for induction in the emerging power structure led some of the important leaders from these castes to pull themselves away from the federation even though it led them to play second fiddle to the upper castes. This suited the interests of the upper caste leaders who appeared disturbed on account of the unity among the members of the middle range castes. The Triveni Sangh lost its strength also due to its failures in delivery of the results that it has promised. Caste orientation failed to camouflage intra-caste class differentiations. *Shudra* politics thus remained wedded to unity within the castes eluding fusion of identically placed castes in some sort of a federation. Competitive politics in the post-Independence phase unleased a process of political modernisation. Castes appeared less important than the ideologically wedded political parties. Some of the concerns of the old caste associations were included in the agenda of political parties. Such limitation of lower caste politics frustrated the emergence of 'an encompassing category' on the pattern revealed in the *Shudra* politics of the south.[28] Secular concerns that facilitated emergence of strong corporate social identity with widespread support did not have pressing presence in this part of the country.

Bihar seems to differ from the states in the south in its crusade against the dominance of the upper castes. Its strategies differed from these states in some respects. It had its own ways to challenge the *status quo* in the traditional hierarchy. Opposition to the dominance of the ritually superior seems to have been led as in other parts of the country by the prosperous and educated upper *shudras*. One important difference lies in its tolerance to the prescriptions enshrined in the Brahmanical social order. The other backward classes of Bihar expressed their resentment against their socio-economic exploitation under the prevailing social order favouring supremacy of the upper castes individually as well as collectively. Sustained efforts to destroy the caste system were, however, never a priority concern in their movements for upward mobility. Upper *shudras* remained superior to the lower *shudras* in spite of the social movements seeking diminution in the dominance of the upper castes. Lower *shudras* and the untouchables have been by and large treated as inferior partners supporting the dominant upper *shudras*.

In Bihar the lower castes were more concerned about their economic exploitation and political exclusion. Culture and ethnicity used by Phule to interpret exploitation of similar social categories in Maharashtra did not constitute the themes in stirrings of the middle range castes of Bihar. While the initial initiatives of the lower castes in the southern and western states opposed the traditionally legitimised religious practices and stressed programmes for educational attainment, in Bihar the mobility strategies of the middle range castes emphasised internalisation of sanskritik values in addition to these secular goals.

Thus, the movement articulating opposition to the dominance of the upper castes manifested sharp differences in the two parts of the country. While in the south and the west of the country it tended to be conflictive it was more or less conciliatory in nature in the north. The uprisings of the middle range castes of Bihar like the other states in the northern parts of the country failed to acquire the degree of institutionalisation evident in similar stirrings in the states with early history of similar stirrings. In spite of differences in the thrust and strategies characterising the *shudras'* movements these seem to have some identical features. In the first place it may be noted that these movements were not initiated by the low and weak among the deprived sections as the dominant and powerful rural castes provided the lead. Another important similarity of such movements in the different states is manifested in their ultimate outcome that also seems to have favoured concentration of power among the sections which held the command and in their unwillingness to facilitate its wider dispersal and downward percolation among the weaker sections of the community.

The proponents of lower caste unease in Bihar did not favour destruction of the exploitative social order. In the quest for parity in status with those occupying the top location, idea for its replacement through a new social order had little importance. The lower castes in Bihar were not inspired by Phule's ideology which placed emphasis on truth, reason and equality for structuring interpersonal relationships among different sections of society. His crusade to discard the religious services of Brahmins whom he considered unworthy middlemen unnecessarily interfering between the people and the supreme had no takers among the lower castes of Bihar. The lower caste stirrings did not suffer from what has been described as 'primordial xenophobia' witnessed in the southern and the western parts of the country where in the course of the anti-Brahmin movements the Brahmins were characterised as "foreigners who had imposed their foreign culture on the indigenous Marathi-speakers and Dravidians."[29]

Shared social privileges and political power among the castes placed at the apex of the traditional stratification system on the one hand and the failure of the inferior middle range castes and the Scheduled Castes to endorse the lead taken by the dominant middle range castes are the factors held responsible for the non-emergence of lower caste movements in the northern states on a scale witnessed in the southern and western states of the country. Competing interest for elevated location in the traditional stratification system tended to be inimical to the unity of the *shudras*. While such sections elsewhere expressed opposition to religious ceremonies that required the presence of Brahmins, in Bihar their preference for internal reform strengthened the value-premises conducive to the maintenance of ritual superiority of the traditionally superior. Oriented to reform within, such stirrings tend to be soft and conciliatory as these are not opposed to hierarchical dominance. It may here be noted that their pursuit to claim 'higher *varna* status' was not to the liking of the upper castes who wanted them remain placed low in the ritual hierarchy.

In Bihar the lower caste movement failed to acquire the sweep and intensity that characterised such movements in the southern part of the country. One fundamental feature that separates it from the other backward classes movement of the south lies in its target of attack. The castes with middle ranking ritual and social positions for a long time in stead of opposing the upper castes preferred to assert ritual parity with them. They provided documentary evidences in support of their claims and made them their reference group of identification for imitation. Significantly, nowhere an attempt was made to hold the Brahmins responsible for the backwardness of these castes. Traditionally endorsed discriminatory practices were there but for their perpetuation individual upper castes were considered guilty. The state of dispersed dominance did not favour targeting of one single caste. The landed exploiting landed interests and parochially inducted placements in the emerging opportunity structure constituted the primary concerns. The other backward classes waited long for the fulfilment of their aspirations that was achieved in the course of their success in politics.

REFERENCES

1. H.F. Owen (1987), "The non-Brahmin Movements and the Transformation of Congress 1921-22" in *Struggling and Ruling* (ed.) by Jim Masselos, Sterling Publishers Pvt. Lted., New Delhi, p. 46.
2. M.N. Srinivas, (1966), *Social Change in Modern India,* Allied Publishers, Bombay.
3. Keer, quoted in H.F. Owen, *op. cit.*
4. M.S. Gore, (1989), *Non-Brahmin Movement in Maharashtra,* Segment Book Distributors, New Delhi, p. 22.
5. *Ibid.,* p. 4.
6. M.S. Gore, (1989), Social Movements and the Paradigm of Functional Analysis, *Economic and Political Weekly,* Vol. 14, No. 17.
7. H.F. Owen, *op. cit.,* p. 47.
8. Eugene F. Irshik, (1969), *Politics and Social Conflict in South India,* University of California Press, Berkeley and Los Angeles.
9. D.A. Washbrook, (1977), *The Emergence of Provincial Politics: The Madras Presidency,* Vikas Publishing House Pvt. Ltd., New Delhi.
10. André Bèteille, (1969), *Castes Old and New,* Asia Publishing House, Bombay.
11. H.F. Owen, *op. cit.,* p. 54.
12. Nicholas B. Dirks, (2004), *Castes of Mind: Colonialism and the Making of Modern India,* Permanent Black, Delhi.
13. André Bétellie, (1969), *The Backward Classes in Contemporary India,* Oxford University Press, New Delhi, p. 86.
14. Uma Ramaswami, (1978), "The Belief System of the Non-Brahmin Movement in India: the Andhra Case", *Asian Survey,* 18(3).
15. M.S. Gore, *op. cit.,* 1989, p. 44.

16. Susan Bayly (2005), *Caste, Society and Politics in India,* Cambridge University Press, Cambridge, p. 238.
17. Ghanshyam Shah, (1991), "Social Backwardness and Politics of Reservation", *Economic and Political Weekly,* Vol. 26, Nos. 11-12, p. 605.
18. H.F. Owen, *op. cit.,* p. 48.
19. Christophe Jaffrelot, (2003), *India's Silent Revolution: The Rise of the Low Castes in North India Politics,* Permanent Black, Delhi, p. 195.
20. Hetukar Jha, (1977), "Lower Caste Peasants and Upper caste *Zamindars* in Bihar 1921-25", *Indian Economic and Social History Review,* Vol. 14, No. 4, p. 550.
21. K.K. Verma, *Changing Role of Caste Association,* National, New Delhi, p. 14.
22. C. Jaffrelot, *op. cit.,* p. 199.
23. Francine R. Frankel (1993), "Caste Land and Dominance in Bihar", in Francine R. Frankel and M.S.A. Rao, *Dominance and State Power in Modern India,* Vol. 1, Oxford University Press, New Delhi.
24. K.K. Verma, *op. cit.*
25. *Ibid.*
26. C. Jaffrelot, *op. cit.,* p. 195.
27. *Ibid.* p. 198.
28. *Ibid.* p. 199.
29. H.F. Owen, *op. cit.,* p. 52.

4

Empowerment Through Protective Discrimination

Society in traditional India represented a context of inequality legitimised under the caste system. It tended to be unfair to the lower castes as it denied them parity of status with the upper castes. The traditional social order did not allow the low castes to acquire skills 'reserved' for the upper castes. This rendered them laggard even in the context that was open and accommodative. Since there was congruence among different attributes of status social inferiority implied economic marginalisation as well as political weakness. On account of the constraints of cumulative resource disadvantage the people located low in the caste hierarchy found it difficult to find placement in the modern opportunity structure. They lagged behind the upper castes who on account of their superior endowments and manipulative skills were in a position to accelerate their lead in appropriating the benefits of development. Such situation produced a context of lop-sided development. Corrective measures were, therefore, required to atone for the sins of the past. Stains of the past had to be washed away through the rectification of the guilt of the exploitative tradition. Hitherto excluded or marginally represented deserved ensured inclusion in the opportunity structure not only to enable them to have "a proper look in to the administration", but to also effect a proper social balance. Among the various steps contemplated for social animation, the policy of protective discrimination is the most remarkable. Enshrined in the Constitution, the policy of protective discrimination comprises especial support provisions to enable the historically disadvantaged groups to integrate themselves with the larger society and its opportunity structure on equal terms with the sections endowed with inherited superiority. It has the intent of upliftment of the socially excluded though selective application of laws and policies in their favour. It seeks to broad base the state power that used to be the exclusive province of the upper castes. It is thus a rectificatory device.[1] It is aimed at providing redemption to the socially retarded from the condition of inherent inequality. Initiated under the British administration it maintains its presence as an essential component of the state welfare strategy in the post-Independence India. Compensatory discrimination is an "estate duty on inherited intangible wealth" earned by the people placed at the apex of the caste hierarchy.[2] Its impact in reconstruction of society has been impressive as it has helped in laying the infrastructure for sponsored upward mobility of the historically disadvantaged. In fact the 'coming up' of the people from these sections from "the lowest estate into which people have ever fallen anywhere at any time in human history" has been feasible through preferment both in education and job.

The measure is not only an important component of the social policy of the socialist state wedded to redistributional ideology, it has in its own way contributed significantly in ushering fundamental alteration in the upper caste dominated power structure in the different states of the country. This could happen with the coming together of the numerically dominant middle range castes who in spite of growing political strength remained underrepresented in bureaucracy and professions. In spite of the existence of provisions for entitlements of reservation benefits to sections not included in the schedules meant for the purpose the government remained oblivious to their need and aspiration in this regard. While the provisions for reservation in favour of the Scheduled Castes and the Scheduled Tribes acquired the endorsement of the government without much effort on the part of these sections of the society, in the case of the other backward classes it required long wait and protracted struggle. Commissions were appointed to study the problem and suggest measures. Their recommendations, however, were not taken seriously. This made these sections especially the middle range castes uneasy. In the clientelistic power structure that kept them as surrogate to the numerically insignificant upper castes they preferred to remain quiet. However, once this unnatural dominance was weakened rendering them politically important the issue of reservation in favour of such sections acquired salience. Their demand for the benefit of reservation facilitated the coming together of different components comprising the other backward classes which in due course of time acquired prime location in the power structure. Since the aspirations for state sponsored mobility has been the most important factor in the emergence of elite from among the deprived sections including the middle range castes, it appears imperative to analyse in historical perspective the state initiatives and public reactions in this regard. Such exercise is important in order to obtain meaningful insight into the changing pattern of distribution of power and privileges among the different components of society. Stresses and strains involved in a context of dispersed inequality witnessed in the wake of introduction of the provisions of reservation deserve elaboration in order to study the consequences of weakening of the traditionally legitimised equilibrium. Its role in emergence of elite from among these communities and dispersal of power and privileges within the section represented by them require special discussion. The discussion on reservation that follows tries to cover these issues.

Provisions for reservation of the backward classes did not have unanimous endorsement in the constituent assembly. There was a section that considered it undesirable as in their opinion it may lead to spread of communalism and strengthening of the caste system. It was felt that such arrangement would discourage merit and would render the system of administration inefficient. Cleavages produced, it was feared, would lead to disintegration and splits in the social order. Among those who did not oppose the provisions there were some who considered socialistic development of society more important than reservation. Others supported the initiatives as necessary steps to remove the inequalities ingrained in the caste system and favoured it for its political necessity. The first Backward Classes Commission was appointed by the Government of India in 1953 and was entrusted with the task of evolving the criteria for identification of deprivation among castes and communities not included under those already scheduled in the Constitution for the purpose of providing special protection. It was not mandated to explore issues of deprivation among individuals as it was established with the purpose to study backwardness among the groups to enable the state "to do away with the hierarchy of caste and its consequent social discrimination, and prepare the ground for full social equality."[3] The Commission prepared its report within two years of its formation and identified 2399 groups as socially and economically backward. It also suggested measures for their upliftment. There were recommendations for reservation in government jobs and educational institutions in the report. These had the endorsement of the majority of members of the Commission. One member of the Commission did not approve the recommendations as he considered it to be of little help for the empowerment of the population whom it sought to make equals to the upper castes. He wanted the commission to reserve seats for the backward classes in assemblies for a period of twenty years to ensure 'snatching away' of power from the upper castes. Others who were not in agreement with the report did so as they wanted more comprehensive indicators for determination of backwardness. Caste status according to them could only indicate little in this regard. It was also maintained that excessive importance to caste would impair national integration and deepen casteism. Kalelkar, the Chairman of the Commission, also opined that backwardness had to be determined for individuals and their families as identification of castes for state support was undesirable in a milieu oriented to the formation of a casteless and classless society. Caste reservation, according to him, had to be avoided to preserve the unity in society and to avoid communalism. He made a plea for reservation in favour of the economically weak from all sections of society. Contradictions thus introduced damaged the very purpose for which the Commission was created. The report was placed in the parliament after eight years of its submission and it carried with it the 'negative note' of the minister of home affairs. On the issue of reservation suggested by the Commission the government's spokesperson maintained that these were "contrary to the Constitution, would perpetuate caste, and would create in the recipients both vested interests and a sense of helplessness."[4] The Government did not accept the recommendations on the ground that the report lacked the methodological rigour needed for identification of the castes as backward. It expressed its disagreement with the criteria adopted as these were neither positive nor workable. Its recommendations were considered unacceptable on account of their destructive implications. Commenting on the recommendations of the Commission, the Government maintained that the criteria of caste violated the 'first principle of social justice' as these were unfair to the other poor. It was also felt that steps for reservation on the basis of caste would accord a fresh lease of life to an institution that was being weakened under the impact of forces of modernisation. The Home Minister to whom the report was submitted maintained that caste reservation would lead to perpetuation of the existing distinctions and would encourage separatism. He also favoured the need for identification of some positive and workable criteria to determine social and educational backwardness.[5] Use of caste for distribution of state support did not get endorsement of the bureaucracy and social scientists. Suggestions were made to identify backwardness using economic criteria. Thus the Study Team on Social Welfare and Welfare of the Backward Classes in 1959 recommended the abolition of the category of OBC and suggested its replacement by economic criteria in identification of beneficiaries for special support from the government. Social scientists emphasised the need for evolving a 'neutral' scale using the indices of literacy, landow-nership and income in cash or grain in identification of backwardness.[6] It was observed that in certain states backwardness was exploited by certain 'powerful groups' to serve selfish interests. It was also felt that reservation in long run leads to dependence proneness making the beneficiaries less self-reliant.[7] The report was also criticised for its expansiveness as barring a few exceptions it seemed to have included the swamping multitude whose presence in the list of groups entitled for special support amounted to the negation of the interests of the more needy. Caste and caste-based reservations were disregarded in favour of economic criteria. Claims for the extension of special redistributive measures to new sections hitherto excluded from such entitlement was so disturbing to the existing power structure that it now emphasised on the trickling down effects of the programmes for economic development for offsetting the inequalities associated with caste. Its emphasis on socialist programmes and concerns for national unity, however, were in reality excuses to mask "the desire to maintain the *status quo*".[8] After its refusal to accept the report the

Centre requested the State Governments to make *ad hoc* surveys to identify the backward classes in order to provide reasonable support to such sections as were listed by them as backward classes or if not listed were educationally and socially backward in their opinion. The State Governments were also asked to accommodate candidates from these sections in such seats in educational institutions as were reserved for the Scheduled Castes and tribes and for which candidates were not available from these communities. In spite of its emphasis on application of income as the criterion for identification of backwardness the Centre evinced little interest towards the formulation of "a workable quantitative standard for selecting backward communities."

Consequently with the refusal of the Central Government to provide an authentic definition of the other backward classes "composition of the OBC, the scope of preferential programmes and the level of benefits" differed from state to state. Since the states were free to have their own list of social categories comprising the other backward classes there were states where the bulk of the state population was included while in some states a thin layer located above the untouchables could find accommodation. In preparing the list some states resorted to economic tests while some others used caste to determine backwardness and in the rest both economic criteria and caste received salience. States also differed in the level of benefits that were made available to these people. Thus even after more than four decades of independence the term 'backward classes' remained conceptually ambiguous and implied different units in different states. retaining 'multiplicity of meanings.' The term included within its ambit "the totality of groups entitled to preferential treatment on the basis of their backwardness." While the castes among the untouchables and the tribals existing in insularity had the endorsement of the Central Government confusion prevailed in the case of the other backward classes as this task was left to the wisdom of the executive in the states.[9]

The appointment of the first Backward Classes Commission marked in a way a milestone for the low caste movement in north India.[10] This provided an occasion to the middle range castes to officially express their unease over the deprivation they had to encounter since time immemorial. Their concerns in this regard comprised the numerous memoranda sent by them to the Commission. Such sections appeared impatient and bitter for their continued degradation. Pre-fixed location in the traditional social order was no longer acceptable. Creative measures to canalised this awakening appeared to be the need of the time. Mobilisation of the other backward classes that ensued on account of the non-implementation of provisions for reservation amounted to the furthering of the non-Brahmin strategy for empowerment in the south to an area that has till then remained a terra incognita in this regard.

In the south caste based quota was in existence at the time their counterparts in the north were organising to press the state for its implementation in their favour. The impact of the Kalelkar Commission, therefore, produced different responses in the two parts of the country. While the southern states decided in favour of increased representation of the middle range castes in the state bureaucracy, the northern states took time to appoint Commissions that could have enabled them to draft schemes to introduce the system of caste based quota. States in the north thus remained slow in taking advantage of the political situation that appeared conducive to such initiatives. Bihar tended to be a laggard state in introducing provisions of reservations. The demand for adequate representation of the middle range castes was first made in the year 1931 when Swayamber Das raised the issue in the legislative council. He maintained that there was no representation of these castes in the Bihar and Orissa Provincial Civil Service. It was dominated by the upper castes especially the Kayasthas whom he described as a privileged caste. He particularly referred to the plight of his own caste (Yadava) in this connection and maintained that out of 134 sub-registrars in 1931 hardly two were Yadavas. He urged for some reservation to ensure the representation of the excluded section of the society. He pleaded for the appointment of a committee of three officials to suggest ways and means to make bureaucracy more socially inclusive. He reminded people of the earlier movements on account of which the upper castes had to surrender claims on certain privileges and hoped that with passage of time similar achievements were expected in many more spheres. His sentiments were endorsed by another member of the council whose interest was confined to secure larger representation of Kurmis the caste to which he belonged. Special support to the socially and economically section not included in the federal list were available in Bihar since 1951. It included Hindus as well as Muslims. Such castes were placed in two categories. The first list included castes in state of extreme deprivation, while those considered superior to them were placed in the other list. These two lists were known as Annexures 1 and 2 respectively. State provided them financial support in the way of educational help. Thus the state conceded limited concessions as it provided only meagre financial support to small number of students from these sections. Existence of a list of the other backward classes and its classification under two categories representing different degrees of social backwardness was perhaps considered enough. Quotas in administration tended to be elusive. Individual initiatives to seek legislative endorsement for reservations in favour of the middle range castes could not succeed on account of the opposition of the upper caste dominated legislative assembly. Thus in 1953 a private member bill introduced by a legislator of the Congress Party had to be withdrawn following instructions from the party leadership. The Kurmi leaders in the party also pressed for such provisions. One of the important leader from this caste, Deo Sharan Singh, made attempts to seek endorsement to proposals of reservation. His initiatives also did not produce the intended results. In 1964 the Patna High Court declared these lists to be unconstitutional as these had caste rather than class as the criteria to determine backwardness. Under this circumstance the State Government in 1971 appointed a Commission under the Chairmanship of Mungeri Lal who was an important Scheduled Caste leader of the state. The appointment of the Commission was also necessitated on account of the changing political scenario that demanded more attention to the interests of the middle range castes. The decline of the Congress Party and the consequent rise of the Communist Party and parties with socialist leanings contributed significantly in altering to a great extent the social profile of the upper caste dominated power structure. The Congress Party after nearly two decades of independence for the first time selected a leader from one of the dominant middle range castes to be the Chief Minister of the State as it wanted to stop the continuing erosion in its support structure. In the fast changing political context its new Chief Minister who was himself a Yadava appointed the first Commission for the

Backward Classes. The Commission encountered immense difficulties in collecting desired information on account of the non-cooperative attitude of the upper caste bureaucracy. It submitted its report in 1976. While identifying the castes for entitlement of reservation the Commission took into account their social status, level of education, extent of presence in the state bureaucracy, and involvement in industry, trade and commerce. It put the other backward classes in to two categories. The report identified 128 castes as socially and economically backward. The castes thus identified as backward were the same that were earlier included in the Annexure. It, however, contained in addition a few Christian groups also. The Commission divided the castes included as the Other Backward Classes in to two categories. 93 castes were named as the most backward castes while the remaining were labelled as the backward castes. The Commission indicated in its report that the middle range castes had sparse presence in the state bureaucracy especially in its upper echelons. It made a plea for their reservation in the state services and educational institutions. It also fixed the quantum of reservation as it felt that 24 per cent of the seats in educational institutions and 26 per cent of positions in state services had to be reserved for these people. The recommendations, it may be noted, were never considered fit for reservation as long as the Congress remained in power in the state. With the change of regime that took place some fifteen years after the submission of the report these were implemented with modifications. In the year 1978 the Janata Government that decided to implement the recommendations of the Commission did not favour identical entitlements for the two categories of the castes identified for state support. Under its provisions castes listed in Annexure 1 were entitled for 12 per cent reservation while those in Annexure 2 were allotted 8 per cent. The reservation policy thus enunciated had provisions for reservation for women and economically deprived among the upper castes making each of them entitled for a share of 3 per cent jobs in the state services. Taking into account the provisions already in existence for the Scheduled Castes and the Scheduled Tribes the extended clientele thus proposed made half of the jobs available in the state reserved for such sections that were considered backward. The reservation provisions introduced by the Janata Government made Bihar the "first state in India to reach the maximum limit set by the Supreme Court."[11] This was a big leap forward so far as the middle range castes were concerned as they tended to be "grossly underrepresented at all echelons of the state bureaucracy".[12] It appeared unprecedented and had not only to encounter violent protests from the upper caste people but also had to witness the demise of the Government responsible for the implementation. Bihar was not the only state to have unfavourable orientation towards reservation of seats on the basis of castes in fact most of the states "displaying the strongest reluctance to reservation policy are in the Hindi belt".[13]

The rejection of the recommendations of the Kalelkar Commission Report did not amount to end of the issue. The report was dropped but not the issue. It was resurrected from what has been described as 'so convincing a death' after a decade when pursuing its electoral agenda the Janata Government appointed a Commission under the chairmanship of B.P. Mandal to look into the possibility of providing reservation to the section not included in the schedules to the Constitution. In fact the appointment of the Mandal Commission represents the first serious attempt to institutionalise reservation for the other backward classes at the Central level. The second Backward Classes Commission was appointed in February 1978 by the Janata Party rulers in pursuance of their declared policy. The Commission was entrusted with the task of evolving a criteria to identify the socially and educationally backward classes and to recommend steps for amelioration of the status of the people thus identified. It was further asked to examine the desirability or otherwise of providing reservation to inadequately represented backward classes in the services of the Central Government. The Commission submitted its report in December 1980. The report expressed its concern over inadequate representation of the other backward classes in public services and made suggestions for their larger inclusion through reservation. It felt that in order to "upgrade the cultural environment of the students" from these communities this was needed. It made a plea for special educational facilities to the students from this social category as it would lead to "upgrading of the cultural environment" in which they are nurtured. Suggestions for skill upgradation of the artisan castes were made. It also expressed the desirability to support the commercial and industrial initiatives through a network of financial institutions. The Commission expressed itself in favour of radical land reform so that the lower castes could find freedom from dependence on upper castes. The suggestions made, however, were not implemented due to the sudden demise of the Government. Efforts to implement the recommendations of the Commission by the caretaker government did not succeed in absence of the consent of the President.

While Karpoori Thakur decided to implement the recommendations of the Mungeri Lal Commission in Bihar to defeat the designs of the upper caste dominated bureaucracy and the upper caste leaders within his own party to unseat him from the Chief Ministership of the State, V.P. Singh implemented the Mandal recommendations to keep himself in power in spite of the distrust of their party leaders in their leadership. These two leaders encountered identical situations and resorted to reservation with the aim to coalesce the lower caste support in their favour. The formula that Karpoori Thakur evolved was, however, more scientific than the formula suggested by the Mandal Commission. Caste tended to be the primary determinant in both of them, however, the former considered the economic status of the individual to be of equal importance in deciding his eligibility for entitlements of reservation benefits. The other distinguishing feature of the Thakur's prescriptions was the endorsement to the reality of inner differentiation within the castes comprising the other backward classes. It arranged not only separate quotas for the forward and backward sections in the middle of the stratification but also fixed higher quota for the poor and more numerous kept in the second category. It also had provisions for reservation for the poor upper castes and women.

The people of India particularly its upper castes were surprised at the Centre's decision to arrange reservation for the other backward classes at the national level. Probably the Parliament's unanimous endorsement to this initiatives in 1982 was not taken seriously and was perhaps taken to be a pious pledge with no intention for implementation. While no political party opposed the provisions the intellectuals appeared equally unconcerned. Such section of people and intellectuals that were "uneasy over the recommendations hoped that parliament would, with the passage of time forget its own unanimous approval and the whole issue would die down."[14] Sudden developments to translate the constitutional pledge on the issue into reality bewildered those who were not prepared for such eventuality.

The Mandal Commission and its recommendations were scrutinised to challenge the appropriateness of extending reservations to the other backward classes. It is maintained that the Commission was biased to favour the middle range castes as it seems "to have made up its mind on the recommendations before it started deliberations" and had "little concern for the expert advice whom it consulted to acquire legitimacy."[15] Thus, it seems to have succumbed to the pressure of least deserving interests ignoring the interests of really distressed. Political pragmatism seems to have favoured recommendations that were scientifically untenable thus institutionalising compensation for personal inadequacy. Social and economic concerns are alleged to have camouflaged political partiality. The report is referred to as a strident political manifesto intended to please the other backward classes for their political support to the outfit in the saddle. Numerically strong middle range castes turned out to be political resources whose welfare found sudden concern in the strategy of the political entrepreneur. They were made to realise that in order to elevate themselves in the status-structure they need to capture state power as imitation of sanskritik values was least effective for such upliftment. Considerations being out and out political parties ignored rationality. On account of the political intentions thus imputed the whole exercise is described as an attempt at restructuring of the machinery of administration to serve the interests of castes that have taken strides forward.[16] The Commission is also criticised for ignoring the interests of the weaker sections among the other backward classes as it does not contain mechanism to ensure downward percolation of benefits.[17] Such arrangement would thus leave the weak and vulnerable to their luckless fate. This lapse on the part of the Commission finds elaboration in the dissenting note of one of it the members who is a Scheduled Caste. In his observations he has noted that certain sections among the other backward classes are not only ritually superior but are more close to the upper castes than such middle range castes who have low numerical strength and are ritually inferior to them. Such dominant sections have significant presence in politics and professions and are likely to corner the major portion of benefits made available under the protective discrimination programme leaving little for the more depressed sections. He pleaded for inclusion of safeguard inputs to prevent lopsided distribution of the benefits. In his opinion there has to be a separate list in the Constitution for the depressed middle range castes. The methodology adopted for the identification of the castes recommended for inclusion in the list comprising other backward classes is criticised for being "erratic, whimsical and politically loaded" deliberately adopted to include forwards among the backwards.[18] On account of their privileged location these upper backward communities are said to be endowed with societal resources in the manner it has benefited their ritually superior. Such castes, it is maintained, do not deserve reservation as they have been partners of the upper castes "in the exploitation of the truly deprived" and bear 'the guilt of the social order' in same degree as the upper castes. Conclusions derived on the basis of unscientific investigations represent 'pleasing fiction.'[19] 'The recommendations are criticised for their intent to accord enmasse extension to the provisions of protective discrimination in favour of the other backward classes." Such enlargement of the clientele of protective discrimination, it is said, would lead to a negation of "the principle of equality of opportunity."[20] In a society seeking to modernise itself through "liberal democracy and economic development" endorsement to provisions for 'proportionate shares' to castes and communities in public employment 'represents/attempts' to invest the caste system with legitimacy by claiming that its constituent units have 'rights and entitlements' and is bound to be defeated in the end; but in the meantime it can cause enormous harm to 'society and its institutions.' Provisions of reservation do not help the landless labourers, small peasants and low wage earners in the unorganised sector. Such families among the target group who have 'land with infrastructure and marketable skill' are better poised to appropriate the benefits.[21] This would in turn compound elitism as it benefits the selected few leaving the poor out of mainstream. These privileged elites while imbibing the life style of the upper castes colleagues find themselves alienated from their own castes. The state's indifference to the interests of large number of people among the upper castes under the new reservation provisions has been criticised.

The report of the Commission is also described as a document prepared in a haste. Completion of its enormous and complex assignment pertaining to the determination of backwardness of the entire Indian population in two years is a short time. Its failure to accord salience to secular and neutral criteria in deciding backwardness is also deplored. Professionals consider it as "direct onslaught on the culture of meritocracy." It is maintained that reservation in teaching institutions produces 'ill-taught students'. One ever persisting objection to reservation is that it compromises with merit and strengthens primordialities as it leads to inefficiency. Extending this argument it is maintained that implementation of the recommendations would lead to further erosion in the efficiency of the administration as "soft corridor of recruitment keeps society deprived of the services of the most competent persons". In this way, it is said, the Commission "lacked a wider perspective" and ignored the "need for an efficient and professional civil service capable of undertaking growingly complex tasks of democracy and development."[22] Upper caste bureaucracy considers reservation to be "retrograde step as it discourages initiative and development and encourages inaction and parasitism."[23]

Hindu outfits consider it a ploy to 'cleave the Hindu community'. Such concerns are expressed in the writings of some social scientists also to whom the latest initiatives for reservation to the other backward classes represent "a tragedy of the highest order and a scheme to fragment a society." Extended clientele of protective discrimination is designed to transform the Indian society on the pattern the pre-Independence non-Brahmin activists in the west and south desired both having identical interests of depriving the upper castes from their privileged location. Plea for compensatory discrimination is being used as a camouflage and a clever cover up to hide the mobility aspirations of the numerically strong and politically assertive castes in the middle of the traditional stratification.[24]

Initiation, perpetuation and extension of facilities inherent in the policy of reservation on the basis of caste for upliftment of the weak and depressed has been widely opposed. It is criticised on the ground that it has rendered non-Hindus unworthy of state protection. This amounted to endorsement of the orientalist outlook on Hinduism that caste is inherent only to this faith and other religion being fundamentally egalitarian in their outlook do not stigmatise any section within its fold as socially inferior to other sections. It, therefore, considered the lower caste fit for the benefits of reservation. This the Commission did even after recognising the fact that caste like stratification prevails among the non-Hindu religious groups. It is also criticised for the method that has been employed to measure backwardness to prepare the list of castes entitled for the benefits. The efforts of the administration in this regard represent "many of the errors and contradictions of the old colonial ethnographic inventories." Consequently, castes selected represent status groupings with differential experience of discrimination and not homogenous communities with an inheritance of uniform disability. The provisions for reservation are also questioned for their failure to be comprehensive in coverage as may individuals from upper castes who are in need of such support than some of the not so needy individuals from the castes availing the state protection are not included. It is also maintained that "far from expunging the evils of caste, they create incentives for Indians to affirm their caste origins since aid-seekers must proclaim ritually inferior birth in order to qualify."[25] In the opinion of the liberal and progressive thinkers the concept militates against the spirit of equality and secularism as it is likely to sharpen the pre-existing social cleavages. Caste is recommended to be kept out of policy prescriptions. Economic criteria is regarded more suitable for the determination of social backwardness.

The political use of the Mandal Commission, it is maitained, would divide society in smaller units separating the supporters and opponents as conflicting social cleavages leading to escalation of sectarian interests. Social fissures thus ensued would serve the purpose of the self-serving interests as such contexts are conducive to their perpetuation in power. The pursuit for social equity through reservation caters to the political needs of the interests wedded to consolidate their hold on communities seeking reservation. In case of sincerity the matter has to be left to those whose interest has been ignored. Prolonged stay of the reservation policy, it is maintained, "blunts the enterprising fervour of even the capable among the backward classes" as such sections 'develop an explicit affinity' to spoon-feeding and loose interest in harnessing their latent potential.[26] The other backward classes are considered least worthy for entitlement of protective support of the state as under this category are included "castes and caste clusters of the rural rich." Notwithstanding the fact that they lack education and are not well represented in state services, they are, however, considered to have 'land and money' that may help them to acquire the social assets that are not presently available to them. Thus, the 'large section' among them who are 'economically powerful' and are 'substantial land owners and cultivators' do not need state support in the form of protective discrimination. Availability of reservation to those who are in possession of socially valuable assets has the "danger of degenerating into a kind of patronage politics which vitiates the quest for fraternity and gives affirmative action rather a bad odour."

Among those who favour extension of reservation to the other backward classes, there are observers who consider this support to be "a short-cut, soft and sly reform measure to cater more to the psychological aspirations of that section of the population which constitutes the majority than trigger a process of a process of radical structural change in society." It is maintained that reservation is in fact a strategy to perpetuate the prevalent in egalitarian structure by conceding accommodation a thin layer of elites emerging from among the erstwhile socially excluded strata in the elite-structure dominated by the upper castes. Reservation is a concession that is aimed at blunting the possibility of emergence of initiatives wedded to fundamental transformation. "In such a scheme of governance, the poor belonging to upper, middle and lower castes have to suffer." The measure notwithstanding its inherent limitations have to be welcome as it is in the interest of a section of the traditionally deprived.

Those who favour reservation for the other backward classes maintain that those who criticise this step on the ground that it will lead to inefficiency ignore the fact that states with long stint of reservations do not have more inefficient administration than those with recent experience in reservations. It is also maintained that help for the Blacks in the United States for coming up in the government sector did not have any perceptible impact on the efficiency in administration. Contesting the undesirability of reservation for its disastrous impact on efficiency the supporters of the policy maintain that in order to ensure fair play to merit the country should open its doors to imported merit.

Under the one party dominance system with the Congress as the sole party of governance the reservation scheme remained 'a politically neutral administrative tool' oriented to arrange succour for the deprived. With the decline in the political clout of the party and on account of the rising political profile of the middle range castes scramble for material and electoral endowments available under the provisions of protective discrimination found new claimants from among the politically ascendant ritually inferior other backward classes. On account of the pragmatic compulsions of competitive politics welfare oriented reservation seems to have lost its credibility as a tool to compensate the traditionally wretched of the country for the injustices of the past. It has ceased to be "a politically neutral administrative tool aimed solely at correcting injustice and relieving deprivation". Extended clientele of protective discrimination represents its 'sweeping version' and seems to transform the Indian society on the pattern the pre-Independence non-Brahmin activists in the west and south desired both having identical interests of depriving the upper castes from their privileged location. Plea for compensatory discrimination, it is maintained, is being used as a camouflage and a clever cover up to hide the mobility aspirations of the numerically strong and politically assertive castes in the middle of the traditional stratification.

In conclusion, it has to be mentioned that its stretched scope might have suited the interests of strong pressure groups, it was, however, necessitated on account of the slow rate of induction of the lower castes in state supported occupational structure. Such situation in fact was conducive to perpetuation of an upper caste dominated administrative structure. The 'merit-based' recruitment policy of the state operated in a manner that on occasions it appeared to be a camouflage facilitating the induction of persons with strong social networks. Manipulations acquired legitimacy in the name of merit as these could arrange favours even for the otherwise undeserving provided there are supporters to push their case. Such scenarios did not spared even the candidates from the upper castes for whom there was no support. But, it more damaged the cases of the middle range caste candidates as there was explicit biased against them. Those who oppose reservation to save merit should also expose the distortions and malpractices that are inherent in the prevalent procedures for selection of people for employment. Similarly, the anxieties for rise in intracommunity inequalities that reservation is likely to produce would not be a valid ground to discontinue its execution. To rid the scheme from such distortions the matter has to be left to those whose interest has been ignored. Such sections, however, have to be properly sensitised to thwart distortions in the policy content as well as the implementation of the programme. Reservation is necessary to have socially inclusive administrative structure. Social justice cannot be sacrificed at the altar of inadequately defined or ill-defined efficiency[27]. In spite of the weaknesses and lapses the provisions favour 'secularisation of the middle classes.' In the process, however, thus contributing to the weakening of the caste system. It is a measure with "tremendous psychological spin off" as members of communities thus elevated feel equal to the traditionally privileged in this regard.[27]

It is also not proper to maintain that opposition to the quota based reservation is on account of the fact that the upper castes consider the lower castes' backwardness to be the wish of the almighty and these castes unworthy of inclusion in the opportunity structure as they lack the requisite merit needed to claim the positions. It would be more appropriate to say that unacceptability of reservation by the traditionally embedded is due to their unwillingness to tolerate questioning of the social equilibrium that has been facilitating their status as social superiors. With the increase in the demand for reservation by new sections and on account of diminishing opportunities leading to fresh threat to their unquestioned supremacy there has been further intensification in their opposition to the state supported schemes of protective discrimination. Reservation has been "an explosive feature of Indian politics". This is but natural in a context where the state happens to be the main employer and large masses from the social categories with inherited inferiority remain excluded on account of constraints in acquiring the requisite skills and also on account of manipulations of the entrenched upper castes aimed at denial of accommodation to persons from the lower castes in the privileged position of administration. In Bihar, for instance, the widespread violence that was triggered in the wake of the decision to provide reservation to the middle range castes was on account of the upper castes' perceptions of reservations for the middle range castes as a threat to the prerogative of the upper castes among whom the employment opportunities used to be shared. The opposition to the provisions also reflected their bewilderment over the courage of the Government headed by one of the most backward caste leaders to offend the interests of the section that had till then unquestioned supremacy in society and administration. In reality also it was made explicit that the emerging social forces were in the process of replacing the upper castes as the locus of power. The decision to reserve jobs was an announcement of this new phase in the politics of the state. Issues pertaining to purity and pollution, places of residence of different castes, occupational specialisations had little relevance as the upper castes were concerned more about diminution of their space in the services under the Central Government. Struggles for reserved seats in state services do not seek destruction of the caste system. In fact these have the intentions to reduce the representation of the upper castes in favour of the 'caste-based deprived social groups'. It has no intent to attempt renegotiation within the hegemonic structure as it seeks to ensure an independent space to the forces in the middle and at the base of caste hierarchy. It is oriented to usher a rearrangement in the state benefits in a manner that suits the interests of the castes placed at lower location in the traditionally legitimised stratification. It does not represent a strategy to ensure alteration in the status structure. The new initiative "brought the anthropology of caste out of the academy and into the forefront of public discourse".

The potential beneficiaries seemed pleasant prepared to offer strong resistance to forces opposed to its implementation. Society seemed split as passions aroused. Social tensions that ensued reflected the response of the people to this unprecedented state action poised to disturb the traditional congruence between caste class and power. While the traditionally entrenched upper castes feared diminution of their share in the prevalent occupational structure, the politically ascendant castes considered it to be a step wedded to their status elevation. Arguments for and against the reservation that followed reflected 'moral passions' suiting the selfish interests of cleavages thus produced. Opposition to affirmative action summarised 'in the language of justice' reflected concern for rights of individuals, while its support favoured the rights of castes and communities.

The manner in which the recommendations of the Mandal Commission was implemented in the states has been described as a strategy to 'punish those defined as upper castes' as the measures looked on those on the outside as responsible for the deprivation of the section of people whom the new schemes sought to support. Such perceptions on the part of the upper castes led to violence on an unprecedented scale even in Bihar. Expansion of reservation net triggered caste hostilities as further erosion in resources of power and influence was unacceptable. Tensions are natural in changes that involve clashes of interests. Cost free solutions to problems seeking structural transformation are impossible. The movements in favour of reservation, its supporters maintained, would complete the fight for freedom that was led by Mahatma Gandhi that stopped once the country attained independence. It would enable the fulfilments of the dreams that the country had envisioned then and would facilitate the inclusion of the excluded as participants in the process of development.

The caste war that ensued the announcement of the implementation of the provisions for reservation for the other backward classes was so widespread and intense in Bihar that the State Government had to declare as 'disturbed' all districts of Bihar, except tribal Santhal Parganas and issued shoot at sight orders in the curfew-bound district of Begusarai and Madhepura. People working were attacked and wounded, railway stations were torched and trains were set on fire. Homes and shops were looted and inmates beaten.

Those who participated in the anti-Mandal agitations were mostly sons and daughters from the lower middle class ignorant of the 'sins' of their forefathers for which now they had to suffer. Their dreams to move up through education suddenly appeared shattered.

Its (Reservation's) introduction and subsequent extension in the favour of the middle range castes is considered "an incremental approach to social change". The issue of widening its ambit to include the middle range castes led the lower castes to federate themselves in a manner that was not seen earlier. The middle range castes coalesced to emerge into an interest group wedded to safeguard their interests. It enabled the large social coalition thus formed to acquire a political identity Its success in making the castes comprising this constitutional category aware of their political might triggered "a second democratic upsurge" resulting in large scale political participation of the people from this section. The issue facilitated the empowerment of the middle range castes that had profound impact as it led to transformation of political structure in the northern states of the country where parties wedded to the interests of the other backward classes replaced the upper caste dominated parties as locus of power.

It is maintained that so far as north India is concerned the Yadavas played the most important role in preparing the middle range castes for sustained assertion in favour of their claims for reservation. In support of such claims, contributions of the top leaders especially from these castes are elaborated. This is, however, only partially correct. In fact, in the enthusiasm to put this thesis the contributions of many leaders, from different other middle range castes have been lost sight of. This is not only unfair, but also presents a simplistic interpretation of the reality. The middle range castes would not have been successful without the support of the then Prime Minister V.P. Singh who initiated steps for the implementation of the recommendations of the Commission that was constituted on account of the pressure of Charan Singh, the Home Minister in the first non-Congress government at the Centre. Ram Vilas Paswan, the Welfare Minister in the V.P. Singh Government, is a Scheduled Caste and he evinced impressive determination in favour of the implementation of the provisions for reservation in favour of the other backward classes. Some of the important crusaders to the cause who were then in power at the state level had to loose their position as were considered intolerable. Karpoori Thakur the most powerful and respected leader of the middle range castes in Bihar was a barber. The students that constituted the core support to the Mandal initiatives in Bihar were mostly Kurmis. Jagdeo Prasad, the Shoshit leader whom his supporters called 'Lenin of Bihar', was killed in a fake encounter for his bold utterances in favour of reservation. He was a Koeri. In Patna, the capital of the state of Bihar, the most crucial role was played by the Kurmi Youth residing in Patel Chhatrawas. So grateful the leaders of the Janata Dal were to these students that on all important occasions they used to visit these lodges in future also. Thus, the success in attaining the long cherished aspiration for reservation in favour of the other backward classes was possible with the support and involvement of different castes and leaders. No individual leader or caste has to be credited for the success.

REFERENCES

1. S.R. Maheshwari (1991), *The Mandal Commission and Mandalisation,* Concept Publishing Company, New Delhi.
2. G. Thimmiah (1993), *Power Politics and Social Justice,* Sage Publications, New Delhi, p. 23.
3. N.K. Bose, (1954), "Who are the Backward Classes", *Man in India,* Vol. 34.
4. MarcGalenter, (1984), *Competing Equalities,* Oxford University Press, New Delhi.
5. C. Jaffrelot (2003), *India's Silent Revolution: The Rise of the Low Castes in North India Politics,* Permanent Black, Delhi, p. 226.
6. M.N. Srinivas, (1957), *Presidential Address to the Anthropology Section of the Indian Science.*
7. Marc Galenter, *op. cit.*, p. 177.
8. C. Jaffrelot, *op. cit.*, p. 229.
9. Marc Galanter, *op. cit.*
10. C. Jaffrelot, *op. cit.*, p. 229.
11. Marcus Frande, *Small is Politics,* Wiley Eastern Ltd., New Delhi, p. 235.
12. Harry, W. Blair (1980), "Rising Kulaks and Backward Classes in Bihar", *Economics and Political Weekly,* Vol. 15, No. 21, p. 66.
13. C. Jaffrelot, *op. cit.*, p. 152.
14. Andrè Bètellie, (1991), *Economic and Political Weekly,* Annual Number, p. 591.
15. A.M. Shah, (1991), 'Double Talk', *Hindustan Times,* 7th September.
16. Meenakshi Jain, (1991), "Irony of the Mandal Commission," *Indian Express,* September 3.
17. S.R. Maheshwari, *op. cit.*
18. S.C. Dube, (1991), "A Retrogade Fetish", *Hindustan Times,* 3 September.
19. Ramashray Roy, (1991), "Fiction into Fact", *Indian Express,* 30 August.
20. Andrè Betellie, *op. cit.*, p. 593.
21. Ghanshyam Shah, (1991), *Economic and Political Weekly,* Annual Number, p. 609.
22. S.R. Maheshwari, *op. cit.*
23. Ghanshyam Shah, *op. cit.*, p. 609.
24. Susan Bayly, *op. cit.*
25. *Ibid.*, p. 277.
26. G. Thimmiah, *op. cit.*, p. 24.
27. G. Thimmiah, op. cit., p. 30.

5

The Other Backward Classes Under One Party Dominance System

The upper castes tended to be the locus of power in pre-Independence Bihar. In the first decade of its existence the leadership in the Congress Party was drawn from the educated upper castes especially the Kayasthas. The Bihar Provincial Congress Committee that came into existence at that time was a constellation comprising professional groups small landlords and tenants.[1] Professional groups constituted the 'principal lieutenants' of Gandhi in his initial years of stay in Bihar. Support for the movement was drawn from small landlords and affluent peasants through whom he could reach to the different villages. Homogenous social composition helped it to maintain its cohesion. The diversification in the support structure in subsequent decades led to the inauguration of the phase of factional politics in the Congress Party. While the upper castes dominated the organisation there was marked shift in the composition of the elite structure in favour of upper castes previously placed at the margin. The supremacy of the educationally superior Kayasthas was challenged by landowning prosperous Bhumihars and wealthy Rajputs who were more numerous than the Kayasthas and had wider spread through out the length and breadth of the State.[2] Each of the three castes competed among themselves for important placements in the organisation and other structures of power. With the passage of time and till a decade after independence this narrow stratum of ritually superior and economically prosperous castes retained its dominance in politics in spite of being split into factions. The middle range castes and the Scheduled Castes remained in a surrogate status. None of these two categories had their independent leaders as the situation favoured their existence as secondary leaders confined to the periphery of the power structure. Such leaders represented "co-opted members of the elite" in the party. The middle range caste leaders in the Congress Party in order to survive had to be the appendage of the upper castes. These sections did not consider it proper to have a separate political party wedded to their own interests perhaps in obedience to the spirit of national unity that was required in the fight against the British. But the main reason tended to be the imperatives requiring individual caste to maintain its separate entity thus minimising the chances of coming together of different castes to assert for corporate interests. This was perhaps also the reason for non-emergence of "a state organisation of Hindu and Muslim backward castes" representing the socio-economic interests common to the weaker sections across caste and community.[3] The leadership in the Congress Party was also against the emergence of any political party representing the interests of the middle range castes and on occasions thwarted such initiatives with the help of middle range caste leaders loyal to the upper castes.

Success of the Congress in 1937 elections unleashed a bitter struggle for the control of the party and has been described as the moment of disintegration.[4] While the upper castes fought among themselves they saw to it that power did not slip down in the hierarchy of caste. Circulation of elite remained restricted within the upper castes. Competing elites in the upper caste dominated Congress Party did not endorse steps unfavourable to the perpetuation of the social equilibrium traditionally legitimised. The dominant castes never consented to rearrangement in the hierarchy. The leading socio-economic and political movements in spite of the support of the lower castes and untouchables consciously remained oblivious to such aspirations. The desire of Gandhi to uplift the impoverished peasants did not have the support of the persons for whom Gandhi was an ideal. On account of the indifference of the so-called cultured men with worldly prospects and political ambitions the task was entrusted to workers from Gujarat and Maharashtra.[5] Such programmes had to be politically pragmatic. Support of the big and prosperous had to be ensured even if it amounted to endorsement to their exploitation of low and deprived. Initiatives for addressing the problems of the small and poor peasants mostly from the middle range castes never received the support of the leadership in the party. The Congress refusal to initiatives against Darbhanga Raj and its unwillingness to support no-rent payment campaign are two of the many instances reflecting its strategy of non-interference in the prevalent arrangement oriented to the prosperity of the zamindars.[6] The poor and low could have organised themselves independently but their faith in the charisma of Gandhi and their proneness to dependence lulled them into inaction. The poor supported the movement for independence even with financial support from their meagre resources, whereas the Congress "did not get much from the rich people."[7] Persons from well-to-do families constituted the support structure of the party. During the elections that were held in pre-Independence period the party did not find it necessary to include even one representative from the lower castes as member of the Bihar Pradesh Congress Committee.[8]

The socialists of the pre-Independence India appeared more serious than the conservative Congress wedded to trusteeship utopia of Gandhi in identifying the priorities to outline the course of social transformation. The low castes were for the first time considered politically significant and socially more deserving to merit attention in the programmes contemplated for social reconstruction. The Congress Socialist Party that turned out to be the nucleus for initiation to Socialism in India expressed its resolve to work for "the elimination of landlordism and the redistribution of land to the peasants". It sought to facilitate fostering of unity between the "lower castes and the masses". Its formation of the Kisan Sabha had the intent of exerting revolutionary pressure on the Congress to force it to evince needed attention to the cause of the peasantry. Caste inequality, however, escaped the attention due to it in the social reconstruction programmes of the Kisan Sabha of the Socialists.

Other political parties also drew their leaders from the same upper castes and had insignificant influence over the state power structure. Some of them especially the Communist parties were ideologically wedded to the plights of the poor and had contributed immensely to rid the landless labourers, share-croppers and workers in the factories from the exploitative clutches of the feudals and capitalists but had least concern to protect the interests of the socially excluded in the emerging opportunities in the new occupational structure. The poor from the lower castes looked at these parties in the time of distress. In fact these masses constituted the support structure of the Communist Party in the state rendering subordination to upper caste leaders. Class ideology thus appeared inimical to the growth of leaders of eminence from the lower castes who could ultimately dominate. In Bihar Communism helped the upper caste leaders especially the Bhumihars to practice politics without impairing the interests of classes to whom they were committed to eliminate. Left orientations in the organised sector of politics in Bihar is reported to have found articulation under the leadership of Bhumihars and such parties are "relatively better organised in areas dominated by this community." Since its foundation in 1939, the state unit of the Communist Party was dominated by Bengalis and Bhumihars. Presence of leaders from other castes that ensued with the widening of its support structure did not affected the dominance of Bhumihars who constituted the real centre of power in the authority structure of the party. While the Bengalis held important positions, the real control was in the hands of Bhumihars. One of the important leaders of the Samayukta Socialist Party, Bhola Prasad Singh once remarked that the CPI was a party of Bhumihars and the Bengalis were its *munshis*. The party that was proud of its secular credential did not favour the elevation of even one non-Bhumihar to strategic positions in the organisation. It betrayed a definite caste bias in favour of the lead caste in the party so far as nominations to Rajya Sabha and Vidhan Parishad was considered. Ramavatar Shastri—a Yadava, who represented the party several times in the Parliament was never considered fit for the position of secretary of the state unit. In the first non-Congress coalition government in which the CPI was also partner, out of the three member representing the party two were Bhumihars while the third was a Brahmin holding the position of State Minister. Later a tribal was also inducted as a State Minister. The party appeared oblivious to the absence of the middle range castes and the Scheduled Castes in the organisation. It is also said that these Bhumihar leaders of the Communist Party defeated the chances of Karpoori Thakur to lead the first coalition and favoured an upper caste nominee, Mahamaya Prasad Sinha—

a Kayastha, who represented the party of Raja of Ramgarh to become the first non-Congress Chief Minister of the State. The leaders in the Congress Party were in close liaison with the communists and socialist parties. Here also the caste of the leader was more important than his ideological leanings.

Caste coalitions, conflict within the party characterised the Congress politics in the years immediately after Independence. Claims for larger share in the power structure made the warring upper caste coalitions oblivious to the forces opposed to its dominance. "In its inimitable fashion the Congress Party of Bihar kept itself engaged more in the politics of power within the party than in the politics of confrontation with Congress opponents."[9] The endemic factionalism in the Congress, however, led to a situation where the lower caste leaders were sponsored to important location to lend strength to a leader who wanted to have an independent power base. K.B. Sahay—a Kayastha, who became the Chief Minister of the State after defeating a backward caste candidate (Bir Chand Patel) with the support of Bhumihars and Rajputs with the intention of carving out an important political base for himself promoted some powerful leaders from the sections who tended to be underrepresented in spite of the numerical strength of their communities in the population of the State. Small numbers of Kayastha legislators and uncertain support of other upper castes were factors unfavourable to the continuance of K.B. Sahay as the Chief Minister of the State. In order to survive and with the intention to raise his own independent support structure he inducted a powerful Yadava leader, Ram Lakhan Singh Yadav, into his cabinet and allotted him an important portfolio. In the same vain a Kurmi, Deo Sharan Singh, was made the Chairman of the Legislative Council. It was in his regime that a tribal occupied important placement in the Cabinet. Under his leadership some of the individuals from these sections emerged so powerful in the Congress that they could influence the affairs of the party in future also. The sponsored inclusion of leaders from such sections as important entities in the power structure marked a new phase in the politics of the Congress Party. Pressure of competitive politics thus made the party more accommodative favouring inclusion of more leaders from the important middle range castes. However, this process tended to be selective favouring those who tended to be conciliatory and were not opposed to the dominant elite structure. Such recruits from the lower castes subsequently acquired more power than many of the leaders of individual upper castes.

The rise of Ram Lakhan Singh Yadav as the most important leader of the Yadavas constituted a landmark development in the politics of the State. His rise indicated that it was possible for the middle range castes to have leaders from their own castes on the pattern of the upper castes. Ram Lakhan Singh Yadava used to be considered the Pope of the Yadavas in Bihar. He remained the most important caste leader of his time and remained quite influential for nearly two decades. On the eve of the 1967 elections his insistence for 60 per cent seats annoyed the upper caste leadership which rejected the suggestion and in their heart of hearts remained uncomfortable to his eminence in the party and to his intentions to favour political rise of middle range castes had ensured cleavages within the upper castes and the lower castes. Upper caste manipulations in the Congress did not favour his further rise in power. The defeat of the Congress in 1967 and the split in the Congress that ensued thereafter changed the political situation. The new leadership that emerged in order to keep the party under the *de facto* control of the upper castes especially the Brahmins promoted a few not so important Yadavas with the specific purpose of keeping him low in the party. This was the time when the socialist were successfully inducting Yadavas and other middle range castes in the party, in the State Legislative Assembly and in the Central Parliament. Now, the Yadavas had many leaders from their caste in the opposition ideologically inclined to lift the *Shudras*. This heralded a process of massive erosion in the support of Yadavas and other castes in the middle of the stratification from the Congress Party.[10]

The most important factor that provided sharpness in the articulation of the intolerable unease among the backward castes against the dominance of the upper castes was the release of the report of the Backward Classes Commission. Its recommendations for reservation of seats in bureaucracy and educational institutions had profound impact on the politics of the middle range castes as it ushered a programmatic shift in their initiatives for upward mobility. Sanskritisation lost its significance as the most important strategy for status elevation as acquisition of secular attributes of status were considered more important. In order to attain these attributes a need was felt to unite identical interests group to form a powerful pressure group. This required political mobilisation of the middle range castes as informal social networking was insufficient. The leaders in spite of a favourable context failed to evolve a federated political community of the castes seeking ascendance. Instead they remained confined to individual castes to which they belonged and limited their activities to their own areas of influence. Upper *Shudras* maintained distance not only with lower *Shudras* but also with the Scheduled Castes. Numerical strength is an important resource of power. The numerically superior, however, has to be politically conscious and has to work unitedly to make the strength of number as the overriding resource. The middle range castes lacked the unity required to replace the upper caste in the structure of dominance. The emerging leadership in middle range castes appeared more concerned to the interests of the upper *shudras* in spite of the support of more poor numerous castes placed below them.

It was Rammanohar Lohia who made people from the middle range castes realise the importance of their numerical strength. Under his leadership a process of mobilisation of the castes comprising the other backward classes acquired an unprecedented success. Not only such elements in the different socialist permutations but those opposing the unnatural dominance of the upper caste dominated Congress Party and till then existing as inert and passive onlookers lent their support to this initiative. Bihar was in the forefront representing a new context and a landmark stage in the political empowerment of the middle range castes. Lohia insisted on implementation of provisions for reservation in favour of the middle range castes as he considered this system of support to be the most appropriate empowerment scheme. Sections opposing reservation were soon marginalised in the party and preferred insignificant existence with ideologically intimate colleagues in different separate political outfits. Many of them were from the upper castes and had a dominant presence in the Praja Socialist Party. 75 per cent of the leaders in the Praja Socialist Party were from the upper castes and probably on this account the party showed little interest to the issue of caste inequality. At the same time some important upper caste leaders who had concern for the middle range castes left the Praja

Socialist Party to work with Lohia. The Samyukt Socialist Party with Lohia as its supreme leader held the overwhelming presence of the upper castes in different political parties partly responsible for the weak organised stirrings for social transformation. It, therefore, not only favoured increased representation of individuals from the lower castes in state legislators and parliament but also in reality implemented its resolve with successful results in the states, the party had strong support base. Bihar described as the cradle and birth place of socialism in India was at the top. Lohia wanted to empower the middle range castes. Since, it was not possible he campaigned for replacement of the Congress Party. He was instrumental in forging a united front comprising different non-Congress parties having diverse political ideologies. He succeeded in his mission. It is, however, wrong to maintain that the Congress was unseated on account of the rise of the middle range castes. In reality unity of diverse interests and irreconcilable fights within the Congress did this miracle. In this process upper castes not attached to the Congress supported candidates from lower castes also. The upper castes in these outfits availed the support of middle range castes aspiring for accommodation in the power structure. People wanted change and relief from the unpopular and corrupt regime that maintained its long presence in spite of popular unrest against it. Such coming together of forces opposed to Congress was the major factor for the emergence of a new set of leadership in Bihar. It would, therefore, be right to maintain that rise of the middle range castes at that point of time was due as much to the negative sentiments working against the Congress as to their intensive mobilisation in many cases under the leaders from the upper castes. In the 1967 elections that produced this erosion in the Congress Party's strength in the legislative assembly most of the important upper caste leaders in the Congress had to face men from their own castes as candidates of the opposition parties. Even K.B. Sahay lost his seat to a Kayastha who succeeded him as the Chief Minister of the State. Once in power the Socialist thought it prudent to ignore the implementation of their ideological priorities. Its new leaders did not appreciate the presence of persons of upper caste many of whom were old Socialists in the party. There developed casteism in a new form where three dominant middle range castes dedicated themselves to the promotion of individual caste interests. It led to a situation where colleagues from different castes were neglected in favour of castemen in other parties. Three ritually superior middle range castes dominated the party and was, therefore, called 'Ahir-Kurmi-Koeri party'.

The first non-Congress coalition government that was formed after the elections witnessed the rise of Karpoori Thakur as the most important leader of the middle range castes. While the collective leadership in his party remained supreme, the implementation of the social empowerment programme was stirred by Karpoori Thakur, a leader who was from one of the most backward castes and had mass following. Not only he had long experience in politics but was also simple and honest. He became the Deputy Chief Minister in the coalition Government after the debacle of the Congress Party and was in a position to extract maximum concession for the social constituencies to which his party was dedicated. His slogan on the unity of backwards and emphasis on the share in power due to them found wide reception among the poor and deprived in Bihar. He urged them to consolidate themselves to strengthen his party as it was determined to arrange for them sixty per cent share in politics and administration (*Socialist ne bandhi ganth. Pichara pave saume sath*). Karpoori Thakur emerged as the most popular leader of the middle range castes in Bihar. His appointment as the Chief Minister of Bihar symbolised the simultaneous consolidation of an alternative to Congress and the political rise of the backward castes. His inability to keep the rising personal interests of his colleagues under check led to a split in his party resulting into the untimely demise of the first non-Congress Government in Bihar.

The coalition that succeeded Thakur Government was sponsored and supported by the leadership in the Congress Party and was headed by B.P. Mandal—a Yadava, who is today more known as the Chairman of the second Commission for the Backward Classes. B.P. Mandal was the scion of a prosperous Yadava family in the Saharsa district. He left the Congress Party to join the Samyukt Socialist Party on the eve of the 1967 elections. He was elected to the Lok Sabha but insisted for a cabinet position in the Coalition Government of the State to which his party was a dominant partner. His lust for power did not have the endorsement of Lohia who wanted him to retain his seat in the Parliament. The clash culminated in the collapse of the coalition.

Mandal who engineered the defection in his party to bring down the first non-Congress government became the first Yadava Chief Minister of the State. The Congress supported him from outside. The manner in which he elevated himself in politics marked a departure from the established pattern. Mandal represented a 'shame' in the politics of Bihar. Though this coalition did not survive long, but it appears that a process favouring the continued dominant presence of the middle range castes in the power structure of the state had been ushered. Castes on the ascendance appeared inclined to transform themselves into interest group to form "socio-political coalitions like the non-Brahmins of south India."[11]

The period that followed was the period of political instability. In the emerging equilibrium of power that favoured the rise of lower castes as rulers of the State the upper caste elite manipulated with the help of the Central Government the situation in a way that none of the Chief Ministers from the intermediate castes and the Scheduled Castes could stay long in power. Politics looked dirty as the clean upper caste elite ignored the niceties in order to redress their frustration. Struggle for power increased the importance of criminals till now lying dormant working for the leaders from behind. "Unfettered and undisciplined political competition brought criminals into the political system. Not only has that trend continued over time, but many party leaders since the 1970s have received their political education in that milieu of democracy by gun."[12] Split in the Congress at the national level had repercussions at the state level also as the upper castes comprising its support structure were also divided in their support to the two Congress parties that came into existence after the split. While the Brahmins, the Scheduled Castes and the Muslims remained with the ruling clique led by Indira Gandhi, the Kayasthas, Bhumihars and Rajputs supported the group led by the leaders having control over the organisation. The middle range castes supported the ruling Congress to provide replacement for the loss it suffered on account of the exit of the three upper castes.

In order to retrieve itself the Congress Party tried to usher splits in the Socialist Party and made attempts for revival of the clientelistic model of support recruitment. The Scheduled Castes succumbed to the allurements on account of small representation of these communities in the first non-Congress Government of the coalition parties. Still there was opposition to the attempts to arrange political rehabilitation of the upper castes in the position of eminence that they enjoyed earlier. Such being the social context, the Congress Party, in order to prevent the opposition coalition parties, endorsed the candidature of a Yadava for the position of the Chief Minister. Daroga Prasad Rai the first Congress Chief Minister from the middle range castes turned more disastrous for the upper castes than its previous Kayastha Chief Minister, K.B. Sahay. He drastically reduced the representation of the upper castes in his cabinet, appointed a lower caste person as the Chief Secretary to the State ignoring the claims of many upper caste seniors and appointed the Mungeri Lal Commission to look into the phenomenon of socio-economic backwardness of the backward classes. Rai had to pay a heavy price for his progressive leanings and was soon removed from the post of Chief Ministership as the Brahmins opposed his presence as their leader. The upper castes were supported in their efforts by L.N. Mishra who was then the rising star of the Congress Party at the Centre. The Congress Party, however, could revive itself in the state politics after some time structuring 'an unequal coalition' of castes under an clientelistic arrangement dominated by the upper castes. The forces released earlier initiating the empowerment of the middle range castes thus appeared weakened in midst of unease and resentment against this manipulated stagnation.

The upper castes' interest remained safe under the Congress regime. Even when the party lost its dominance some other parties explicitly wedded to serve the interests of the landed were there to take care of them. The presence of Socialists and Communists did not matter much to them on account of indifference of these outfits towards the plight of the deprived and discriminated sections that constituted their support structure. These parties in spite of the radical intents proclaimed did precisely little to lift this section from the morass of degradation. Changing composition and socio-political profile of the ministries have not affected the interests of the landed class. The provisions that existed on the statute book were left unimplemented. On several occasions the Chief Ministers were from the middle range castes and the Scheduled Castes. Their rise, however, did not indicate the political supremacy of the lower castes. Instead it represented a strategy of the faction ridden upper caste elites who due to their failure to find unanimity in favour of any upper caste leader selected such persons as their 'compromise candidates'. These Chief Ministers constituted the apparent centre of power while the real power remained under the control of the upper castes. This is not to suggest that the lower castes were politically unconscious. Political awareness was there and instincts to emerge as replacements to the entrenched elite were discernible especially among the upper *shudras*. However this could happen only in the late seventies when under the leadership of Karpoori Thakur they succeeded in securing implementation of the quota facilities in their favour. There was thus a good deal of time lag between political awakening and the acquisition of real political power.

The 1967 elections have been described as 'critical one' in the sense that it altered the contours of power structure in India. It heralded the demise of the one party dominance system. A system of competitive dominance appeared in offing. It marked the beginning of a break with the past as previously excluded lower caste occupied significant space in the centres of power. It was witness to a situation where groups were seen involved in 'rewriting their basic loyalties'. These transformatory shifts acquired further articulation in the elections of 1977. The tendency towards dispersal of political power initiated in 1967 was more marked this time. The political developments of the seventies that favoured wider accommodation of the middle range castes in the power structure of the State is often characterised as the struggle for power involving the 'new capitalist kulaks' and the old 'feudal order'. It is also seen as an important consequence of the prolonged assertions of the lower castes to end the unnatural socio-political dominance of the numerically sparse upper castes. The newly acquired prosperity through commercial cultivation and rising representation in politics led the middle range castes to seek commensurate accommodation in the state-controlled opportunity structure. Since this tended to be the privilege of the upper castes there was widespread opposition to demand for reservation.

The 1977 elections were held in an extraordinary situation. It followed a brief stint of national emergency that was clamped to protect Indira Gandhi from the onslaught of the opposition against her continuance in power after being declared unfit to be a member of the Parliament. She decided to remain in power in spite of the disqualification. Emergency was promulgated apparently to 'stop slide towards anarchy' and to contain 'the dominance of permissive politics' in the country. The power that she thus ensured for herself was not based on consensual authority but on the dictatorial control of the civil power. The opposition parties or the dissidents within were not in a position to influence or challenge the regime that had strong presence of illegitimate centres of authority. Under the prevalent authoritarian set up change appeared impossible as no scope was left for conflict resolution. With almost all the personal as well as political opponents of Mrs. Gandhi in jails and the dissidents inside the margin of pressure demoralised, the rulers remained ignorant with the explosive reality at the grassroots. On January 18, 1977, she made an announcement to dissolve the fifth Lok Sabha relaxing the emergency regulations and urged the world's largest electorate "to get to the polls with the resolve to reaffirm the power of the people and uphold the fair name of India as a land committed to the path of peace reconciliation and progress." Common suffering during the emergency gave the protesting parties a cause for unity. United opposition parties pandered the feeling against the Congress. Abrogation of basic liberties, compulsory sterilisation, brutally executed slum clearance and indiscriminate arrests of leaders and activists made people unhappy with the Congress. In order to provide combined opposition to the Congress a party comprising important non-Congress outfits was formed and was named Janata Party. It represented working coalition of disparate opposition parties different with each other in ideology, preferences and social base seeking articulation of peoples' ire against the excesses of emergency. Its political aim was to defeat the Congress Party in the elections that ensued. In the states where such resentments were intense and wide it produced remarkable political results as evidenced in the rout of the Congress Party. Its emergence as replacement to the Congress was to "reverse the authoritarian usurpation of democratic power" as it was mandated to restore the constitutional regime of the pre-emergency era.

The rise of the Janata Party was the result of the political developments of which Bihar was the nucleus. The problems of the state and the failure of the government to address the grievances produced widespread dissatisfaction. Earlier the State had witnessed a long spell of political instability. The Congress Government that was in power cared more for its survival than for the sufferings of the people. Under the press of the circumstances, the students of the State taking inspiration from the student movement of Gujarat turned poised to seek fundamental reconstruction of the socio-political contours of the State. The protest movement acquired importance as its command was taken over by Jayaprakash Narayan who offered to lead a country-wide movement against corruption and authoritarianism. JP questioned the legal and moral authority of Mrs. Gandhi to rule the country. His political experience, skills and stature provided new strength to the movement as political leaders and student activists had immense faith in him. With his efforts it was possible to unite inherently opposed elements for objectives that were laudable. This unity was not to oust some castes out of power but to create an infrastructure that could sustain democracy and freedom and which could ensure social transformation. It was not for replacing 'Tweedledum with Twedledee', but for strengthening the roots of people's democracy. His initiatives produced immense impact in spite of the 'contradictions and lapses' indicated in some of the studies of the movement.

The rise of the middle range castes in the state legislators in the post-Independence Bihar has been most remarkable in the situations where the forces opposed to the Congress were united. Under these circumstances even the upper castes not satisfied with Congress have supported the candidates from the middle range castes affiliated to the parties determined to throw it out of power. Such coming together was rare and was possible on occasions where there was mass public discontent. The JP movement represented one such context. Politically it provided an opportunity to the middle range castes and the upper castes being marginalised to work together in spite of the earlier opposition to each other. There took place a temporary alliance between leading politicians of the Backward classes and their rivals among Bhumihar, Rajput and Kayastha groups all of whom have been excluded from power by Mrs. Gandhi's Brahmin-led coalition."[13] The student organisation known as the Bihar Chhatra Sangharsh Samiti that was formed under the guidance of JP and was the lead organisation in the movement was dominated by the upper castes.

While the upper *shudras* supported the movement, the Scheduled Castes and Tribes evinced least interest.

Students and leaders associated with the movement subsequently turned out to be important entity in the politics of the State and the Nation. Many of the present day leaders including those from the middle range castes in the non-Congress and non-Communist parties owe their origin to the JP movement. The most significant fall out of the movement was the further strengthening of the role of the middle range castes in politics. This could happen in spite of the large presence of the upper castes as participants in the JP movement. It would, therefore, be naïve to ignore its contributions in restructuring the power structure of the State as it favoured the sections who were kept at the periphery in spite of their number and on account of the manipulations of the clientistic politics.

In the elections to the Bihar Assembly that took place after the emergency the Congress Party was defeated and the Janata Party won with overwhelming majority. The other significant development that took place was the emergence of the middle range castes as the most numerous component in the winning outfit. With the support of this section Karpoori Thakur was made the Chief Minister. The upper caste aspirant Satyendra Narain Sinha was not accepted as the Chief Minister was to be elected from among the clique led by Charan Singh. His claim of superior support was ignored by the component to which he belonged. JP also preferred Thakur. In spite of the fact that Thakur had the overwhelming support of the legislaors from the middle range castes but at the same time it has to be noted that his rise to the position of Chief Minister was possible only with the help of many upper caste legislators. It was the spirit of the JP movement that made him acceptable to the legislators from different castes. However, Thakur considered it as an endorsement to the uprising of the middle range castes under his leadership. He considered it as a "mandate to pursue an entirely unrelated policy initiative"[14] that was oriented to empower the lower castes by increasing their representation in his cabinet and provide them larger share in state controlled economic opportunities. "Power came to Thakur first, and the attempt to mobilize and unify the backward castes followed. Although it might be argued that that is somewhat of an exaggeration, the situation was not the other way round."[15] His cabinet included more middle range castes than the upper castes. The upper castes leaders in the party were not happy with the overrepresentation of the middle range castes in the ministry and its pro-Backward policies. However, they had to tolerate it under the instructions of the national leaders who were keen to preserve the unity of the party. Attempts at destabilisation of the Janata government in Patna would have "shaken loose the foundations of the Janata government in New Delhi as well".[16] Thakur also implemented the Mungeri Lal Commission's recommendations with modifications. This triggered violence on an unprecedented scale. With the split in the Janata Party, Thakur had to go. He was succeeded by Ram Sunder Das—a Scheduled Caste Socialist leader with intimate liaisons among the landed castes of Bihar especially the Rajputs. In his ministry the upper castes had the most significant presence relegating the middle range castes to narrower space.

Thus, the squabbling upper caste elite in the Congress Party while contributing to its decline made it possible for some leaders from the lower castes to avail their due in the changing power structure. Outside the party also parties rising with the support of the of the middle range castes turned more efficacious resulting in their wider representation in the legislative assembly. Cleavages between the upper castes and the lower castes acquired sharp articulation for the first time in the political history of Bihar. The Naxalite movement also contributed significantly towards the empowerment of the weaker sections including the poor in the middle range castes. It also for the first time led them to violently question the socio-economic and political clout of the entrenched upper castes. Such factors appeared facilitative to a situation where the prevailing confluence of caste, class and power could be disturbed. The corporate status dissonance that was produced in its wake deserved redressal favouring alterations in the status structure.

REFERENCES

1. G. McDonald, (2006), "Unity in Trial : Congress in Bihar 1929-39", in *Congress and the Raj* (ed.) D.A. Low, Oxford University Press, p. 204.

2. Chetkar Jha, (1967), "Caste in Bihar Politics", *State Politics in India,* (ed.) Iqbal Narain, Meenakshi Prakashan, Meerut.
3. Francine R. Frankel (1993), "Caste, Land and Dominance in Bihar", in Francine R. Frankel and M.S.A. Rao, *Dominance and State Power in Modern India,* Vol. 1, Oxford University Press, New Delhi.
4. *Ibid.*
5. Rajendra Prasad quoted in Francine R. Frankel, *op. cit.,* p. 70.
6. Stephen Henningham (1982), *Peasant Movement in Colonial India,* Australian National University, Canberra.
7. Rajendra Prasad, quoted in Francine R. Frankel *op. cit.,* p. 73.
8. Ramashray Roy, (1970), "Caste and Political Recruitment in Bihar", in *Caste in Indian Politics* (ed.) Rajni Kothari, Orient Longman, New Delhi, p. 242.
9. F. Tomasson Jannuzi, (1989). *India in Transition,* Orient and Longman, Bombay, pp. 17-18.
10. Christophe Jaffrelot, (2003), *India's Silent Revolution: The Rise of the Low Castes in North India Politics,* Permanent Black, Delhi.
11. Christophe Jaffrelot (2003), *op. cit.,* p. 269.
12. Kohli, Atul (1992), *Democracy and Discontent,* Cambridge University Press, New York, p. 214.
13. Francine R. Frankel, *op. cit.,* p. 103.
14. Harry W. Blair, (1980), "Rising Kulaks and Backward Classes in Bihar", *Economic and Political Weekly,* Vol. 15, No. 21, p. 69.
15. Atul Kohli, *op. cit.,* p. 221.
16. Harry W. Blair, *op. cit.,* p. 69.

6

The Other Backward Classes as Locus of Power

Caste has strong presence in the politics of Bihar. The caste pattern of its electoral behaviour has been a consistent feature. People had no reluctance in using caste for political ends. They did not wait until Independence to mobilise caste groups for securing power. In the initial period the power structure was loaded in favour of the upper castes. "In a situation of cumulative inequality the middle range castes and untouchables remained attached vertically to their upper castes patron by bonds of loyalty."[1] Enhanced competitiveness in politics that ensued, however, favoured increased participation leading to wider dispersal of power and pluralism. The traditional elites were weakened as the era of 'appendage politics' characterising the one party dominance system weakened.

Elections of 1990 in Bihar represent a watershed. It unleashed a process of reconstruction of political alignments and support structures. The new alignments in the main friction-points in the society were radical and unprecedented. It appeared that a context reflecting political renaissance was in offing. It marked the eclipse of the one party dominance system. Unprecedented transformation in the elite structure ensued with the overwhelming presence of social categories earlier occupying secondary status in the power structure. It also heralded a phase that favoured the empowerment of the middle range castes. It made it possible for the previously marginalised groups to register significant presence in the corridors of power. Such context was conducive to the presence of parties wedded to local aspirations. The period was important also as it was witness to the birth of a strong state-level party. Lalu

Yadav emerged as the most successful and effective architect of an ideological consensus emphasising social justice and secularism. His determination to stick to the priorities even at the risk of division made him charismatic. With his efforts "the middle range castes emerged as a cohesive force endowed with a psychological sense of identity pitted against the dominance of the entrenched castes."[2] The Muslims saw in him a sincere supporter capable to safeguard their interests. The marginalisation of the senior lower caste leaders in the Janata Dal that followed resulted in the emergence of new leadership that was young. Nitish Kumar was one of them. His rise helped the party to have considerable influence among his castemen, the Kurmis. Nitish became "the second in command of Lalu in the Janata Dal." This was an unique development as it facilitated for the first time the unity between these two castes with long history of rivalry. The two together contributed significantly in weakening the dominance of landed upper castes in many parts of the State.

The issues and programmes that acquired priority under the new regime were favourable not only to the upper *shudras,* these also attracted the Scheduled Castes and weaker middle range castes towards the Janata Dal. Such sections saw in it the possibility to arrange for them redemption from the traditionally legitimised feudal exploitation of the upper castes. The process of marginalisation of the upper castes that ensued made it possible for them to have long cherished social empowerment. Lalu's success in weakening the dominance of upper castes made him the darling of lower castes and dalits whom this section exploited and insulted in the past. Their long time tormentors were now being paid in the same coin. It was, however, not the only the attraction of the programmes and the support of the deprived that lent sustenance to the regime. Lalu in order to survive engineered defections in different parties to keep himself in power. He dented the support base even of the left parties as some of the supporters especially Yadavas deserted the outfits for selfish political interests and also on account of their discomfort in the company of castes lower to them in the hierarchy. Erosion in the support of the left parties was also on account of their 'unqualified eulogy' to Lalu Yadav as the leader of the masses comprising the lowest depths of poverty and social deprivation. Commenting on the decline of the CPI one analyst attributed it to its frequent surrender in elections to parties having better political support. Its concern for immediate political dividends forced it to turn a nelsons eye on the ideological rigours to which the party was wedded. The CPI and the CPI(M), it is maintained, on account of their strategy of electoral tailism, have turned into "flabby parliamentary formation trailing behind this or that party of the bourgeoisie for immediate electoral gains". Even the BJP was not spared as a section of the legislators left the party under the leadership of Inder Singh Namdhari who was after some time accommodated in Lalu's cabinet in lieu of his support to Lalu Yadav.

The period also brought into open initiatives for ethnification of the party system as aspirations were aroused on caste lines. Earlier this tended to be camouflaged as explicit use of caste was discouraged. It now became open and direct. The change thus witnessed marked "a take-off to a political situation wedded to sharp cleavages."[3] While the party representing the interests of the middle range castes appeared determined to push the agenda favouring those whose support it sought, such parties that were traditionally associated with the upper castes left little space for candidates from the middle range castes in the list of party candidates. This notwithstanding in the parties supporting the upper caste interests impact of the new wave in politics was evident as efforts were made to increase the representation of the middle range castes at least marginally. Even the Communist Party of India that had the dominant presence of the upper castes especially in its leadership suddenly inducted one of its old guard belonging to the middle range castes as its state secretary. It also considered it prudent to have electoral alliance with Lalu in order to retain its presence in the state. Its separation from the outfit represented by Lalu earlier resulted in its defeat on a scale that was not experienced before. In fact this could happen because the CPI was loosing the support of the Yadavas who remained committed to Lalu. Lalu was the first leader to have commanded so much support of the Yadavas. His effectiveness in raising a power structure where the upper castes were relegated to an inferior location prompted the Scheduled Castes to support him as he could ensure them redemption from the rapacious clutches of the upper castes. The Muslims had immense confidence in his capacity to strengthen the secular contours of politics.

The success of the Janata Dal facilitated the emergence of a new leadership from these castes, however, it did not lead them to close ranks to challenge the ascendance of the middle range castes. The rise of the middle range castes was the result of their unity which had the intent to resist the forces opposed to the implementation of the Mandal Commission. The disaggregated and status deprived middle range castes had to coalesce in favour of the provisions arranging for them wider space in the state services. Inclusiveness thus ensured to defend the provisions for sponsored inclusion in bureaucracy enabled them to aggregate and integrate electoral and interest group support. The solidarity thus forged was soon ruptured on account of the intra-segementary struggle for dominance and due to the propensity to split' that characterised such initiatives in the past. Conflicting aspirations of 'the natural leaders' of the castes on ascendance led to emergence of counter alliances with fluid political options. Perceived self-interests produced purposive alignments in some of the cases with the socially incompatibles. Initially, it appeared that the outfit that emerged in the wake of mandalisation of politics has the ultimate objective to weld individual castes located in the middle of the hierarchy in to common cultural community. However, it soon appeared that it was nothing more than a purposive get-together of discrete interests operating as a unit for the attainment of political gains. The pre-existing social cleavages that were rendered dormant in the wake of required unity to resist opposition of the upper castes against the implementation of the recommendations of the Mandal Commission soon manifested on account of the numerically superior castes' efforts to appropriate the political dividends to itself. While the various axes of polarisation enmeshed themselves in party the leader got himself disproportionately elevated. The leader aspired to emerge as the supreme outdistancing its rivals. After ensuring stability in the party, Lalu declared himself to be the supreme commander of the party. He took calculated steps to oust those who refused to accept him in the new role. The most significant strategy employed by him was to declare in public the emergence of the MY (Muslim-Yadav) alliance of which he himself claimed to be the leader. This was not expected and was not liked by some of the leaders of the party. He appeared determined to isolate the Koeris and Kurmis by ignoring their important leaders. Nitish Kumar opposed Lalu's initiative to form this new core group ignoring the fact that it had support not only of the different middle range castes but also the entire Muslim community and the *dalits*. He described him as 'a casteist and a neo-Brahmin' with the intention of providing supremacy to his own caste—Yadava leaving others at the periphery.[4] Intolerance to conciliation made the party susceptible to splits. Thus, the Kurmis that were an influential component of the Janata Dal felt slighted for being treated as inferiors to Yadavas who made it clear that they (the Kurmis) cannot claim the same respect and command as their own leader. Non-availability of even 'political pay-off' for the political investments incurred by the non-Yadav dominant middle range castes led to a situation that favoured the party's disintegration. Events soon caught up with the Janata Dal to make its split imminent. The formation of the Samata Party comprised leaders that were hurt and slighted once Lalu consolidated his leadership. The party had the dominant presence of Kurmis and Koeris. Nitish Kumar led the split that subsequently attracted many other leaders not happy with the Lalu's style of politics. In essence it comprised the better off among the bullock capitalists alienated from the power structure they helped to emerge. Initially, it appeared to be a contingent formation separated from the ruling clique under the press of circumstances. In the course of time, however, it acquired strength to emerge as counter point to the Janata Dal. Perceived self-interests forced it to seek affiliations to further its political interests. In its anxiety for survival it sought alignment with Koeri dominated CPI (ML). This opportunistic coming together of the ideologically divergent interests failed to produce the intended political dividends. Their coalescence in to one entity proved to be a damp squib. These did not fare well even within their presumptive ethnic base. Subsequently, the Samata aligned with the BJP with the intentions to federate the forces opposed to the Janata Dal and the Congress. The alliance turned so effective that "in a very real sense it filled the political space opened by the weakening of Lalu Yadav's dominance."

While retaining the support of the Hindutva supporters the BJP emerged as the substitute to the Congress Party as it attracted widespread upper caste support. The upper castes disillusioned with the dismal performance of the Congress Party pinned hopes in the BJP whom they considered more competent to serve their interest and could restore to them their lost glory. The BJP made attempts to transform itself into a party that was open to different castes. The Samata with its strong support base among the Kurmis and Koeris compensated the deficit that the BJP would have suffered on account of its proximity to upper castes. Keeping in view, the irreconcilable differences and ideological differences between the two parties there always lurked the possibility of separation of the BJP from the Samata Party. However, the alliance sustained under the compulsions required for political survival of the two parties. The BJP in particular moderated itself by keeping in abeyance its agenda on Hindutva. The two parties had independent support base. While the Samata was dominated by the middle range castes especially by the Kurmis and Koeris, the BJP represented the interests of the upper castes. Coming together of the two parties has made it possible to build an effective support structure. This is evident from the analysis of the social profile of candidates sponsored by the two parties in different elections. While drawing sustenance from separate catchments the ultimate picture that emerges is that of an outfit that is more inclusive to social diversities than the outfits opposed to it. This electoral partnership has produced rich political dividends. The Samata has been more conciliatory to the upper castes than the outfit led by Lalu Yadav.

The consolidation of the forces fostered to press the implementation of the Mandal Commission further weakened as cleavages multiplied. This happened with the removal of Lalu Yadav from the party after he was implicated in the fodder scam case. Lalu formed his own party and named it as the Rashtriya Janata Dal. Samata also became JD(U) after its merger with a section of the Janata Dal. Each of these splinters of the original Janata Dal while retaining the Mandal umbrella appeared determined to push the others out. It was natural as each tried to have a model of dominance where internal competition had to be discouraged. The parties became subservient to the leader. This notwithstanding there has been a constant increase in the numbers of legislators in the parties wedded to the interests of the other backward classes.[5]

In the year 1967 the middle range castes had 82 members from this social category. Their strength increased to 93 in the mid-term elections of 1969. In the elections of 1972 lower castes failed to maintain this trend. In the elections that were held in 1972 the middle range castes had a diminished strength as only 77 members from this social category were declared elected. In the next election that was held in the year 1977, after the termination of the period of national emergency, the middle range castes once again accelerated their lead as 92 members from their rank were declared elected. Since then there has been continuous increase in their numerical presence in the State Assembly. The middle range castes had 96 members in 1980. This was reduced to 86 in 1985. Their strength increased substantially in the year 1990 as 117 persons from the middle range castes were declared elected. This was the time when the components of this section displayed unprecedented unity to press for the implementation of the provisions of reservation. The solidarity thus forged sustained subsequently also. The middle range castes had impressive success in the year 1995 when the elections were held under the charishmatic leadership of Lalu Yadav. As many as 160 members from this social category found representation in the State Assembly. In the elections that were held in the year 2000 there was once again marginalisation in their strength as only 121 persons from this social category were declared elected. In 1990 there was one outfit claiming to represent the interests of this section and it had 124 MLAs. In the year 1990 the party increased its strength to 164, while the newly separated outfit could get only 6 seats.

The analysis of the strength of the middle range castes in the lower house of the parliament indicates that it has been rising since 1962 when 11 persons from this section were elected from Bihar. It was a big leap forward as in 1952 and 1957 the figures in this regard were of the tune of 6 and 5 respectively. The elections of 1962 inaugurated a trend that favoured increased representation of this social category in the subsequent elections also. The period ranging between 1967 and 1989 represents a phase of marginal increase in the strength of the middle range castes from Bihar in the Lower House of the Parliament. The figures available in this regard are indicative of this trend. Table (*see* Appendix 3) indicates that the middle range castes sent 13 persons to the Lok Sabha in 1967 while the figures for the year 1971 and 1977 are 13 and 15 respectively. The strength of this section suffered a decline in the next two elections to the Parliament. In the elections that were held in 1980 and 1984 the middle range castes of Bihar got success in only 12 seats. In 1989 their condition once again changed and the candidates from this social category were declared elected in 18 parliamentary constituencies. The period that followed could be described as the most impressive in the unity and empowerment of the middle range castes of Bihar as in the three parliamentary elections that were held during this period the middle range caste candidates were declared elected in 24 constituencies. Ten years of impressive success was followed by a phase of decline in the strength of the lower castes. In the 1999 and 2004 elections the representatives of these castes could succeed in only 19 and 15 constituencies respectively.

The social coalition crystalised in the wake of implementation of provisions of the Mandal Commission had to its credit an impressive achievement—the removal of upper castes as locus of power. Caste thus 'provided the Indian masses with the tools of social change: a social unit that was able to create new horizontal solidarities, simply because it was the criterion for politics of positive discrimination, it proved to be an effective means of questioning vertical, clientelistic linkages.[6] Lower ranks in the ritual hierarchy is no longer inversely related to high location in the power structure as the prevalent congruence of power, wealth and superior location in the caste hierarchy has been disturbed and the middle range castes who are ritually inferior to the upper castes are the locus of power in contemporary Bihar. Political ascent of the middle range castes has reduced 'the preponderance of the upper caste peasantry in state politics. Their growing influence has to some extent forced the upper caste peasantry in Bihar to shift themselves to "professions, industry, trade and government and commercial jobs."[7]

Shift in locus of power, however, seems to have favoured the dominant and well-off among the middle range castes. Empowerment that ensued in the wake of Mandalisation has mostly favoured the "forward non-twice born communities" as downward dispersal of power remains elusive. Numerically strong, economically comfortable and ritually superior castes in the middle of the stratification system are more privileged than the lower *shudras*. Their significance derives in part from their numbers, in part from their control over small and medium holdings and in part their relative standing in the caste hierarchy.

Comparative prosperity and numerical strength enabled these castes far better placement than the untouchables and tribals to assert for dominance in the power structure. Among the upper *shudras* the Yadavas have remarkable success in politics on account of their "numerical strength characteristic combativeness and stronger caste cohesion." The dominance of the Yadavas in the power structure is not due only to their demographic weight. It has been possible through the clever manipulation of a situation that favoured removal of the upper castes from their position of dominance. Their success in politics has led to marginalisation of numerically sparse and economically weaker castes comprising the other backward classes. This is not that was sought to be achieved in the ideology that was wedded to unity among these castes for social transformation. It is maintained that such orientation to selfish political interests by the Yadav leaders amounted to betrayal of Lohia. Caste was used to unite the middle range castes for attainment of a specific interest. Once the purpose was served and the upper castes lost their strength the numerically superior thought it prudent to ignore the real intentions in such upsurge.

Uneven distribution of power among the different units comprising the other backward classes is an important issue that deserves attention. The information collected indicates that the four numerically dominant and ritually superior castes have more representation in the institutions of power than those with lower numerical strength and located below these castes in the traditional hierarchy. Among the upper *shudras,* the Yadavas are politically most important as compared to them the remaining three do not have that political stature. So far as the State Legislative Assembly is concerned, more than half of the seats occupied by the middle range castes have Yadavas as the representatives. Next placed are Kurmis and Koeris. If the figures for these two castes are collated they emerge equally politically relevant. Separately seen the rise of one of the two castes seems to lead to a decline in the fortune of the another. It is also evident that the rise in the political status of the middle range castes has favoured the Yadavas most. Their performance has been most impressive in 1995 immediately after the consolidation of power favouring Lalu Yadav. The Kurmis and the Koeris in spite of the favourable political context could not be that successful as excepting on a few occasions their strength remains confined to the phase preceding the emergence of the lower castes as the locus of power. The castes known as the most backward used to have negligible presence in the State Assembly earlier. The political rise of the middle range castes seems to have facilitated their ascendance especially of the two castes, namely Kewat and Mallah. However, these two and a few other among these castes represent the fringe of the power structure. The large majority comprising this social category do not have even symbolic presence. The picture remains similar in the case of the representation of the middle range castes at the national level. The inability of caste to slip downward in the hierarchy of caste thus seems to be a permanent reality.

Similar is the predicament of the lower social stratum among the Muslims. In spite of the emergence of a power structure wedded to more representation to the Muslims that comprised its important support base there was little increase in their strength in the legislative assembly. In fact their number decreased. The Muslims failed to maintain the position available to it in the elections immediately before the phase heralding the ascendance of the middle range castes. This community had the most impressive presence in the assembly in the years 1980 and 1985. The Muslims lost this strength in the year 1990. The number of the MLA from this community was reduced from 31 to 17. There was some improvement in their strength in the elections that were held after five years. However, the community was not lucky to improve its lot in the manner the lower castes had done. In a way it suggests that in spite of massive support from this community the ruling outfit left it placed as surrogates that had no other option. Not only this, it also ignored the interests of the low in the stratification of the community in the way the Congress had done. The new regime under the leadership of Lalu Yadav and his wife may be remembered for dispersal of power among the deprived castes from the Hindu community, but in the case of the Muslims it did not facilitate even this limited dispersal of power. Only a few from this section could find place in the different cabinets formed in the post-Independence Bihar. According to a study during the period ranging from 1952 to 1999, out of 106 ministers appointed from this community 78 (73.6%) were 'Forward Muslims'.[8] The pattern of representation initiated under the one party dominance of the Congress prevailed even after the demise of the party. The study quoted above further maintains that the 'backward Muslims' have low success in the eleven Parliamentary elections that were held between 1952 to 1996. Only two 'Forward Muslims'—Sheikh and Syed—had been more successful than others. The different political parties that competed for Muslim vote have been more generous to the 'Forward Muslims' than the 'Backward Muslims' in selection of candidates for elections. Thus in the 1995 elections to the Bihar Assembly the Janata Dal could nominate only eight 'Backward Muslims' as its nominee, while the 'Forward Muslims' got 20 seats. The Congress Party that included largest number of Muslims in its list of candidates for the election the majority of the candidates (30) were from the 'forward' section while those occupying inferior location in the hierarchy had to be satisfied with only 12 seats. In the Samata Party the figures of the two sections was 18 for the 'forward' section and 6 for the 'backward' ones. The CPI nominated four 'forwards' as its nominees leaving one seat for the 'Backward Muslim'. Politics thus seems to have ignored the interests of those placed low in the community's ranking. The study has quoted one instance where through slight modification in his name a leader from one of the lower Muslim communities could impress others as a 'Forward Muslim' and availed political status that was otherwise denied to the members of his community.[9]

In spite of the constraints and lapses on the part of the leaders credited with the empowerment of the middle range castes the extremely backward castes have been the recipients of benefits not available to them earlier. Thus the lower *shudras* first emerged as a distinct social entity in the wake of implementation of the provisions for reservation in favour of the other backward classes as desired by the Mungeri Lal Commission. Karpoori Thakur made the initiative causing unease among the upper stratum of the middle range castes. He had to pay a heavy price for it as he was defeated by a Yadava who was nominated to contest the election on the ticket of the Congress Party. He had the support of the upper castes also. This category comprises 108 castes and account for 33 per cent of the state population. While Karpoori Thakur helped them to emerge, Lalu Yadav made them stand on their own. Persons from this social category were nominated to different positions in institutions under the control of the State (*see*

Appendix 8). Lalu increased the quota of reservation meant for the most backward castes. Earlier it was 10 per cent of the jobs available. This was first raised to 14 per cent and subsequently to 18 per cent. The raise in the quota immensely benefited the people from this social category as it could arrange substantial presence for them in the state services. Lalu, in fact, converted the support of lower backward castes into a movement for social justice.

The middle range castes emerged numerically strong in the Panchayati Raj Institutions. An analysis of the caste-wise break-up of the representatives elected to different positions at the grass–roots institution for governance as given in Table (*see* Appendix 7) indicates their emergence as the most powerful group. Among the Chairpersons of the Zila Parishad 45 per cent are from this social category while the corresponding figure for the upper castes is 35.2 per cent. No person from the Scheduled Castes could be elected to hold the position of the Chairperson of the Zila Parishad as there was no provision for reservation for the people from this community. This section, however, has considerable presence in the Panchayats as members. Of the total strength of the members elected as members the representation of the Scheduled Castes is of the order of 16.9 per cent. The upper castes control 25.3 per cent of the membership in the panchayats. The middle range castes are more numerous as compared to the two sections, their strength as members being 42.1 per cent in this regard. Among the *mukhias* 45.7 per cent are middle range castes. The Scheduled Castes do not have much success in election for this most important post in the Panchayati Raj Institution as there are only a few persons from this social category to hold the position of the *mukhia*. The upper castes also failed to match the middle range castes in this regard as their strength in this regard is of the tune of 34.0 per cent. Among the middle range castes also the Yadavas appear to be the most successful in capturing power in this rural institution for democratic decentralisation. The Kurmis stand next to the Yadavas. The Koeris who have been equal to the Kurmis in contest for power at the macro-level of power structure are not that successful in capturing positions in the rural power structure. They have been elected *mukhias* in a limited number of cases, but as far as their representation as members and Chairpersons is concern they are more close to the Scheduled Castes. The most backward castes have the lowest representation as members. Their position is by and large similar to the Scheduled Castes excepting the fact that they have slightly more representation as the Chairperson and *mukhias*. It is thus evident that the dispersal of power that has been triggered in the wake of empowerment of the middle range castes have led to a radical reconstruction of the rural power structure also. The alteration ensued have favoured primarily only one caste among them. While the Kurmis are next to them, the Yadavas have the most impressive success. The Scheduled Castes and the most backward castes have identical location in the institution for democratic decentralisation in rural Bihar the failure of Koeris to emerge as a match to the Kurmis is surprising.

The RJD inherited the JD legacy in Bihar. The BJP-Samata alliance retained its upper caste vote but expanded its vote base among other communities and also broad-based its class appeal. The Samata-BJP alliance took the upper class vote while the JD showed a clear lower class support.

Competition for acquisition of power seems to be confined to three permutations. While the upper castes are out to rehabilitate themselves in the power structure the middle range castes are equally poised to retain their newly acquired clout. The segments empowered in the wake of Mandalisation of politics are now fighting among themselves for supremacy in the power structure. This is reminiscent of the faction centred politics of the upper caste under the one party dominant system. The middle range castes in this process have to compete among themselves as well with upper castes. The Rashtriya Janata Dal of Lalu Prasad Yadav in Bihar that is 'the single biggest splinter' from the Janata Dal in the north has the Yadavas as its primary star zone, while the outfit led by Nitish Kumar has the Kurmis-Koeris as its nucleus. In the process, social identities have acquired sharp polarisation. Partisan identities seem to have proliferated in the wake of fierce competition for support. The manipulation of social resources for wielding power has turned out to be the fundamental impulse. The support bases of the dominant claimants for power seem to be socially determined. There is intimate rapport between party alignment and caste identity. Each political parties has separate social identity. Competition for power is articulated in the idioms of caste. The caste underpinnings of rival political forces are transparent. Politics thus seems to have sharpened social polarisation. Stress on caste, however, is not indicative of assertion of ritual superiority. It has rather an ideological issue component manifesting perceived group interests. In a context where secondary associations are least effective resort to primary groups are taken to attain political gains. Secular-associational concerns find articulation in apparent proliferation of the parochial symbolism. Universalistic values of democracy stand in close rapport with primordial instincts. What appeared to be a struggle between castes was in fact represented the competition among different social groups for their 'due' in the power structure. Sharp social polarisation has led to the emergence of highly aligned party system wherein groups are most effective for support recruitment. In this stage of political modernisation 'imperatives of modernity in politics and society' are being mediated through "collectivities and adaptive structures based on birth and integrated by primary group sentiment and interest". Pragmatic concerns of competitive politics seems to have weakened the importance of issues seeking promotion of confessional identity and programmes. While the politics of social pluralism in spite of being favourable to the numerically strong and politically cohesive is however not opposed to empowerment of the weak and unorganised.

The Scheduled Castes in Bihar do not have a party exclusively wedded to its interests. Ram Vilas Paswan, who is the most important leader of these sections, have more ambitious agenda. He joined politics as a socialist. On formation of the Janata Party he was made minister at the Centre. After that he affiliated himself with the other splinter groups of the Janata Party. His rise was not liked by the outfits dominated by the middle range castes. Such parties tolerated only those who could accept inferior position. This made him to have his own party that was mostly controlled by his family members. In a bid to carve out a powerful niche for himself he once tried to have an alliance of Bhumihars and Paswans (Dusadhs). This was called BAP that was to compete with the alliance of Yadavas and Muslims (MY). On rendered unworkable he tried to have Muslims with him. This also did not work. It may here be noted that in spite of having identical orientations Paswan never thought it proper to have collaborations with Mayawati. Thus even the strong numerical strength of the *dalits* has not enabled them to convert their number strength in to effective political power. They remained fragmented and supported different parties committed to the agenda of social justice.

The caste bias of the different political parties is indicated in the selection of candidates in the different elections. We have such information on the social profile of candidates nominated to contest elections by the different parties in the Assembly elections of 1995. The Janata Dal nominated Yadavas in 87 constituencies. Its next preference was for the Muslims who contested in 33 constituencies. Between the Kurmis and the Koeris the Janata Dal preferred the Koeris who were the nominees of the party in 19 constituencies. The Kurmis in spite of being 'suspects' got party tickets for 11 seats. The upper castes had the lowest representation in the list of the party excepting the Rajputs who were to contest in 11 constituencies. The party appeared negatively poised to the presence of the other three upper castes as these had the lowest number of candidates selected to represent the party. The lower *shudras* and the *Banias* in spite of their considerable presence in the State did not receive the priority that they expected to get. Thus the upper castes were accorded lowest priority in the list of the Janata Dal candidates even less than the Muslims and the lower middle range castes. The Samata list of candidates had clear preferences for the Kurmis and the Koeris. Between the two the Kurmis had the lion's share (45). The Koeris were preferred for slightly lower number of constituencies as had their nominees in 36 constituencies. Slightly more in number were the candidates from the Muslim community as 14.3 per cent of the Samata Party's nominations went in their favour. However, as stated earlier the 'backward Muslims' were not so lucky as the section with superior pedigree in allotment of the ticket of this party also. The party appeared more generous than the Janata Dal so far as allotment of seats to the candidates of the upper castes is concerned. The Rajputs were the most numerous among the upper caste candidates of the party being nominated to contest in 44 constituencies. The figures for the Bhumihars and the Brahmins are of the tune of 26 and 23 respectively. The Kayastha were marginally preferred as they got nominated to contest in only 5 constituencies. The Banias and lower middle range castes got nominated in 39 constituencies. The Yadavas did not receive the priority attention as this caste had strong inclination in favour of the Janata Dal. The Samata Party had only 11 Yadavas on its of list of nominees contesting in 4.2 per cent of the seats. The next important party happened to be the BJP. It reflected strong bias in favour of the upper castes. The Rajputs were the most numerous among the different categories of candidates for which we have the details. These were nominated to contest in 44 constituencies. Next in number were the Bhumihars which had their nominees in 41 constituencies. The Brahmins found nomination in 29 and the Kayastha in 6 constituencies respectively. Thus out of 238 seats contested from the non-reserved constituencies 120 went to the upper castes. Among the middle range castes the Yadavas found more favour than the Kurmis and the Koeris. It nominated 23 Yadavas, 16 Kurmis and 15 Koeris as the party candidates. The Banias and the most backward among the lower castes contested in largest number of unreserved seats. It seems to have favoured them more than the lower *shudras*. The Muslims have the lowest representation in this party. The social profile of the candidates of the Congress Party is similar to those in the BJP with a difference that the former is more inclined to the Muslims than the latter. It appears that both outfits were competing for the support of the upper castes.

The three parties that were perceived as the parties of the middle range castes secured 178 seats in the elections to the State Assembly held in the year 2000. The newly formed Rashtriya Janata Dal secured 123 seats while the Samata won 34 seats and the remaining 21 seats were went to Janata Dal (U). Such parties also increased their vote percentages during this period. None of the three outfits were, however, in a position to claim the full heritage of the Janata Dal.

The reservation issue that turned out to be a social leveller forcing the different middle range castes to ignore their differences and forget their mutual antipathies for the attainment of larger social goal has been the main polarising factor in the contemporary politics of Bihar. The unity that it helped to foster heralded unprecedented strides to tackle the inadequacies in political representation by reconfiguring the contours of state politics in a manner that accorded dominant space to the subalterns. No party can now afford to ignore the support of dominant backward castes. The rise of the subaltern elite is evident in their large scale presence in the grassroots institutions of democracy. The figures available indicates power shift in the favour of the middle range castes and *dalits*. It is to be noted here that the middle caste uprisings in Bihar has been manipulated to further the interests of the Yadav elites. In Bihar the low caste mobilisation was used first by B.P. Mandal to promote the Yadavas as superior among the inferior lower castes. Similar intentions can be discerned in the efforts of Lalu Yadav who used the united strength of the middle range castes forged in the wake of the implementation of provisions of the Mandal Commission to promote himself as their supreme commander. His initial targets were the upper caste leaders who initiated the crusade to end the dominance of the Congress Party. In a way they played the most crucial role in promoting the middle range castes as politically significant entity. His next targets were the leaders from other middle castes with clean image and ideological commitments who could have been a threat to his unquestioned leadership in future. With his emergence in politics even the champions of the backward caste movements from his own castes lost their importance. This resulted in weakening of the collective identity of the lower castes that was at its pinnacle at that time. Urge to retain supremacy subsequently led to weakening of the unity of the middle range castes. This is natural in a setting where important dominant castes aspire for independent political space. Differences over distribution of state benefits also leads to dissatisfaction. Personal incompatibility ran deep so far as leadership among the two mega middle castes are concerned.

Polarisation of social forces that ensued did not appear unfavourable to strategic conciliation. Since contradictions within the sections comprising the other backward classes are sharp and often irreconcilable, these outfits are not averse to the sections replaced in the wake of their ascendance. In the quest for power the forces wedded to social justice seem to entertain elements whom they seek to replace. Such compulsions of politics lead to a situation where ideological rigour and party discipline are on the wane as alignments tend to be in constant flux. Ideological priorities have been relegated to a secondary position in the coalitions comprising incompatible interests. Such tolerance for accommodation of conflicting interests has, however, contributed significantly to the electoral success of the individual parties comprising the coalition. Success in politics now favour the existence of coalitions as durable functional reality. Partners with distinct support base coalesce to lend elements of complementarities in the alliance. The need for electoral support from heterogeneous constituencies do not favour exclusion as support has to be recruited from every section comprising the electorate. This notwithstanding different castes have differential preferences in the parties. Caste in its new form, however, seeks to articulate the rising aspirations in politics. The collectivities and adaptive structures based and integrated by primary group sentiments and interests are attuned to suit the imperatives of modernity in politics. Universalistic values of democracy stand in intimate rapport with the parochial instincts. One significant fall out of ıhe split in the dominant middle range castes that was subsequently institutionalised through the formation of contending parties is reflected in the increased importance of the least represented castes located below these castes. Such castes are being mobilised for cooption in the way the dominant middle range castes were included in the Congress Party earlier. With emergence of dominant middle range castes as the new patrons the weak and sparse have to depend on them in the clientistic politics. This notwithstanding the contemporary politics has favoured the inclusion of the ritually inferiors in different institutions of democracy. The ehinification of the party system has immensely contributed to the functioning of democracy as it has resulted into the empowerment of the lower castes. It has diversified the flow of benefits distributed by the state in favour of inferior social categories. Political empowerment of the subordinate ethnic categories has rendered the state more accessible to members of these categories. Sense of efficacy and entitlement has risen. Increased political participation of people at the margin of subsistence may help emergence of an outfit representing their interests. This is, however, no guarantee to some radical changes favouring them.

In spite of its comprehensive and long political tenure the leadership in the ruling outfit is least inclined to people oriented politics. It preferred to sideline the leaders that arranged support for them and in many cases were their sources of inspiration in politics. It remained "high in image building and low in performance." Its achievements have been more symbolic than tangible. The issues of development were ignored in the politics that emphasised social identity. It was the success in replacement of the entrenched that ensured its sustenance in spite of the fact that the regime of the poor displayed least enthusiasm to provide specific policy support to the marginalised. The failure of the caste oriented politics to initiate structural change notwithstanding has "strengthened the legitimacy of the Indian democracy" as it has made it possible for the state benefits to have downward percolation to favour the previously excluded sections.

REFERENCES

1. A.K. Lal, (1995), *Mainstream,* March, 11.
2. *Ibid.*
3. A.K. Lal, (1995), "Caste and Politics in Bihar." *Journal of Social and Economic Studies,* Vol. 13, p. 86.
4. *Pioneer,* 5th February, 1995.
5. *See* Tables on this and other facets of politics in the Appendices.
6. C. Jaffrelot, (2003), *India's Silent Revolution: The Rise of the Low Caste in North India Politics,* Permanent Black, p. 385.
7. *Times of India,* February 14, 1980.
8. Ali Anwar, (2005), *Mashawat Ki Jung,* Indian Social Institute, New Delhi.
9. *Ibid.,* pp. 154-55.

7

Summary and Conclusions

The lower castes' movement featured in the northern India in the early twentieth century. Soon after independence it started getting momentum. This was the time when the states having early start in *shudra's* uprising seem to have established these sections as the most dominant forces.

The social contexts that facilitated the rise of the lower castes in the states considered pioneer in this regard were different from the context prevalent in Bihar. The most important feature that separated these states from Bihar was the concentration of socio-administrative resources in a single caste— Brahmin, that was also the architect of the principle of social differentiation. The middle range castes of Bihar initially sought a change in the traditional systems of social relationships to secure equality with the upper castes. The upper *shudras* had their own caste associations separately spreading consciousness among the individual members. While each of these castes has their own leaders and programmes the ultimate objectives and strategies tended to be similar. Each caste association pressed for superior location of the caste in the traditional stratification system. In this process the larger objective of federating for identical interests remained a casualty. Political collaboration among the different castes tended to be elusive on account of competitive endeavours for superiority in the ritual status. Caste considerations weakened the chances of coming together of different identically placed castes to seek share in the emerging opportunity structure as was the case with *Shudras* in some other parts of the country. Their failure to reform the system in their favour led them to take resort to other measures. Instead of acquiring symbols of superior status they now sought larger command and control over resources that could provide them better placement in the status structure. This represented a shift in their strategy from reform oriented change to transformatory change. In Bihar in spite of rigidity in the social stratification none among those placed at the apex was considered as outsiders and invaders. Such was not the case with the protest movement of the middle range castes in other parts of the country especially those in the south where Aryans constituted the negative reference group deserving condemnation.

Under the one party dominance system, power tended to be concentrated at the apex of the caste hierarchy. Castes with superior social pedigree while competing among themselves did not favour its downward percolation. Bihar represented a social context where power married better with wealth and ritual superiority than with number. Since the attributes of status congrued together to formulate corporate status categories politics reflected the interests of the superiors in the caste hierarchy. Castes in the lower echelons remained surrogate to the upper castes. Lower castes and economically weak groups were like the service castes having low stakes in the prosperity and privileges of the upper castes. Such contexts were inimical to the promotion of equality to different constituents in political participation. Unity in the Congress Party in one party dominance system thus legitimised the existing pattern of social inequality. Contrary to the situation in the south where the non-Brahmins struggled for wider inclusion in the emerging opportunity structure the lower castes of Bihar sought elevation in their position in the traditional stratification through internilisation of upper caste beliefs and practices. The middle range castes competed with each other in claiming superior location in the traditional hierarchy. This weakened the chances of their emergence as single cohesive entity capable to question the dominance of the upper castes. Their attachment with separate factional interests in the Congress Party also minimised the possibility of integration among the horizontally proximate middle range castes. Opposition was not only weak but also disintegrated wasting its strength in opposing each other. The middle range castes in spite of having representation in different parties and in spite of being in significant number remained at the periphery on account of their failure to coalesce their strength in favour of their own rule.

Competition for space in the power structure that earlier used to be confined to the upper stratum of the traditional stratification system acquired a new dimension as it marked the inaugural of a phase of competition between the previously embedded and the recently raised leading to intense polarisation of the society. Weakening of the elite-structure traditionally legitimised and rise of the middle range castes has made the numerically strong deprived communities important as without their support it is difficult to wield power. Changed power mosaic characterised by a shift from 'simple apex-bottom power relations' to 'complex apex-middle bottom power equation' has facilitated wider allocation of power in favour of the deprived. Once the traditional structure of power was disturbed, cracks emerged within the coalition that replaced the outfit uprooted. Conflicts within the other backward classes that characterise the state politics is indicative of a tendency for splits and fragmentation as 'coherent political organisation' favouring the middle social order tends to be elusive in the long run. Ascendance of the middle range castes seems to have made numerical strength and social cohesion more important resource of power than social pedigree. Competitive politics thus has made traditionally legitimised rank order less relevant. Political federation of identically placed social categories favours shift in power from the numerically weak and internally divided upper castes to numerically superior middle range castes. Mobilisation of the middle range castes in the wake of political modernisation thus renders stratification based on ritual rank less relevant for political power and social interaction.

Transformation in power structure has been facilitated on account of the support of the poor and deprived to whom the new permutation appeared to have the intent and potentiality to fulfil their long cherished aspirations. These people who continued to be exploited in spite of the promises of equality, whose organised protests to seek economic reforms brought negligible relief, to whom politics meant continuance of the *staus quo,* supported the federated initiatives of the leaders close to their traditional status in the hope of finding a new social order. Unfulfilled aspirations for social equality and upward economic mobility found articulation in support for the emerging permutation of power.

The other backward classes now occupy the most important political space in state politics. The Rashtriya Janata Dal is the most favoured of the middle range castes. Next in priority is the Janata Dal(U). Parties wedded to upper caste interests continue with their efforts to accord importance to the middle range castes. The middle range castes as a whole, however, refuse to align with any outfit that wish them to accord secondary importance. The dalits and minorities favour alliance with the other backward classes ignoring their early preferences for the Congress Party. Contradictions inherent within might have intense competition leading to weakening of unity formed earlier, however, the middle order is capable to emerge as unified interest group in event of threat to the cause of the socio-political constituency it represents. Transfer of power in favour of the middle range castes has led to division in most of the parties on caste lines.

Power and privileges are no longer concentrated among the upper castes as the upper shudras have been successful in ensuring their downward percolation. Ritual superiority has lost its importance as resource of power as stratification based on ritual rank are less relevant for political power and social interaction. While inner contradictions within the middle range castes persist their rise in politics has resulted in the decline of power of the upper castes. Such situation is conducive to collaboration of the other backward classes with the Scheduled Castes as these two sections are equally opposed to the rehabilitation of the upper castes in the power structure.

Politics is in intimate liaison with the traditional structures. Parties are structured around social core of members to which they represent. Manipulation of caste for political interests is an instance. In the process, however, the structures interacting with the forces unleashed in the democratic setting seems to have acquired new features that are inimical to their traditional character.

Changes unleased in the wake of rise of the deprived sections of the communities seems to have questioned the legitimacy of the ideology of status legitimised under the traditional stratification system. Caste-based exploitation is on the wane in the present context of dispersed inequality. Values rooted in traditional texts and sacred practices have underwent rapid erosion as coercive sanctions facilitating inequality encounter stiff resistance from the recently raised. It marks the inauguration of a phase that seemed poised to unprecedented restructuring of the socio-economic contours of power. Changing power structure has unleashed forces of change inimical to the continuance of the social order traditionally legitimised. Old feudal arrangement has been weakened as the pattern of domination prevalent since long stands eroded. Sense of dignity and weakening of status disabilities ensued in the wake of cohesion among the numerically strong deprived communities has transformed the society in general and the rural society in particular, from a quasi-solid state into a fluid state impinging upon those social structures of the system which continue to exploit and oppress the masses. The other backward classes have now replaced the upper castes in the institutions for democratic decentralisation. They outnumber other social categories. Many other institutional structures wedded to growth and resource distribution are under their control.

Positions in bureaucracy are no longer the exclusive privilege of the upper castes. Social prestige, economic privileges and political power associated with bureaucracy are now available to the middle range castes and dalits as the beneficiaries of the measures of reservation. Provisions for reserved accommodation in the state bureaucratic structure seems to have lent sense of dignity and provided opportunities for economic upliftment of the middle range castes.

In spite of the changes the bulk of the lower castes work as landless labourers and sharecroppers. Migration to urban centres is to seek more working days and better wages. Their representation in white-collar jobs tends to be meagre. Upper castes and superior *shudras* are better poised to appropriate the options made available under the modern economic initiatives. Diversification of occupation is more the feature of the traditionally privileged upper castes and the superior *shudras* than the resourceless lower *shudras* and the lowest among the low Scheduled Castes.

Lopsided empowerment has made the least politically efficacious to depend on outfits that appear to be the most effective option. The most backwards endorse forces that could arrange for them important space in politics and society. The Muslims support parties that could ensure protection from the communal forces.

APPENDICES

Appendix 1

The OBC Population according to the First Backward Classes Commission

States	Total Population (1951)	Estimated Population	% of OBC Population
Assam	9,043,707	2,865,934	31.6
Bihar	40,225,947	15,321,746	38.1
Bombay	35,956,150	11,009,745	30.6
Madhya Pradesh	21,247,533	7,902,586	37.2
Madras (incl. Andhra)	57,016,002	12,680,945	22.2
Orissa	14,645,946	1,356,373	9.3
Punjab	12,641,205	2,565,087	20.2
Uttar Pradesh	63,215,742	26,010,161	42.6
West Bengal	24,810,308		9.1
Andhra		Added in Madras	
Hyderabad	18,655,108	13,766,090	73.8
Madhya Bharat	7,954,154	1,936,980	24.4
Mysore	9,074,972	5,963,902	65.7
PEPSU	3,493,685	442,397	12.7
Rajasthan	15,290,797	3,431,326	22.4
Saurashtra	4,137,359	1,216,475	29.4
Travancore-Cochin	9,280,425	912,272	9.8
Ajmer	693,372	297,699	42.9
Bhopal	836,474	294,534	35.2
Himachal Pradesh and Bilaspur	1,109,466	315,101	28.4
Coorg	229,405	63,727	27.8
Delhi	1,744,072	317,906	18.2
Kutch	567,606	201,170	35.4
Manipur	577,635	35,490	6.1
Tripura	639,029	69,432	10.6
Vindhya Pradesh	3,574,690	1,376,307	38.5
Andaman & Nicobar Islands	30,971		–
India	**356,829,485**	**113,510,830**	**31.81**

Source: Report of the Backward Classes Commission, Vol. III, pp. 14-15.

Appendix 2

The Population of 17 Major Castes and their Relative Share in the Total Population of Bihar as a whole in 1931 Census

Sl. No.	Castes	Population	Percentage of the total Bihar population
1.	Ahir	34,55,141	11.02
2.	Brahman	15,40,306	4.91
3.	Rajput	13,70,338	4.37
4.	Kurmi	13,57,302	4.33
5.	Koeri	13,01,473	4.15
6.	Dusadh	12,84,398	4.10
7.	Chamar	12,55,689	4.00
8.	Bhumihar	8,94,657	2.85
9.	Dhanuk	5,47,308	1.75
10.	Kahar	5,24,030	1.67
11.	Kandu	5,06,384	1.61
12.	Mallah	4,59,560	1.46
13.	Hajjam	4,56,779	1.45
14.	Kayasth	3,68,431	1.18
15.	Pasi	1,72,061	0.55
16.	Dom	1,51,621	0.48
17.	Halalkhor	20,742	0.07

Source: See (1) Harry W. Blair, "Rising Kulaks and Backward Classes in Bihar—Social Change in the Late 1970s", *Economic and Political Weekly*, January 12, 1980, pp. 65-66.

(2) Francine R. Frankel, "Caste, Land and Dominance in Bihar" in Francine R. Frankel and M.S.A. Rao (1993), *Dominance and State Power in India*, Oxford University Press, Delhi.

Appendix 3

Caste Composition of the Members of the Bihar State Legislative Assembly (1967-2000)

Castes	*1967*	*1969*	*1972*	*1977*	*1980*	*1985*	*1990*	*1995*	*2000*
Yadav	37	47	35	51	46	47	63	86	64
Kurmi	14	12	20	21	20	12	12	13	12
Koeri	13	13	8	6	12	18	18	27	22
Baniya	13	16	8	10	13	9	18	18	12
Total (a)	77	88	71	88	91	86	111	144	110
Nimn Shudra									
Kahar	1	–	1	–	–	–	1	3	1
Dhanuk	2	–	1	–	–	–	–	1	2
Tatma	1	–	–	–	–	–	–	–	1
Nai	1	1	1	1	1	1	–	1	1
Malaha	–	2	1	–	2	2	2	1	4
Bhat	–	–	1	–	–	–	–	–	–
Kharwar	–	1	1	1	–	–	1	1	–
Nuniya	–	–	–	1	2	–	1	2	1
Badhai	–	–	–	1	–	–	–	–	–
Gangota	–	–	–	–	–	–	1	2	1
Kewat	–	–	–	–	–	–	–	4	–
Rajwar	–	–	–	–	–	–	–	1	–
Paneri	–	1	–	–	–	–	–	–	–
Total (b)	5	5	6	4	5	3	6	16	11
Total (a+b)	82	93	77	92	96	89	117	160	121
Brahmin	32	28	39	20	37	30	27	9	8
Bhumihar	36	36	44	40	39	38	34	18	19
Rajput	54	50	48	55	38	46	41	22	26
Kayastha	11	8	5	9	6	4	3	7	3
Total	**133**	**122**	**136**	**124**	**120**	**118**	**105**	**56**	**56**

Source: Srikant (2005), *Bihar Mein Chunav,* Vani Prakashan, New Delhi, p. 36.

Appendix 4

Caste Composition of the Lok Sabha Members from Bihar, 1952-2004

Castes	*1952*	*1957*	*1962*	*1967*	*1971*	*1977*	*1980*	*1984*	*1989*	*1991*	*1996*	*1998*	*1999*	*2004*
Yadav	1	2	6	7	9	8	5	8	10	13	13	8	8	12
Kurmi	3	2	2	1	2	1	1	–	3	5	2	3	3	1
Koeri	1	–	–	–	1	3	4	1	4	4	3	5	4	1
Baniya	1	1	3	4	3	1	1	2	–	1	2	3	1	1
Kahar	–	–	–	1	–	1	–	–	–	–	–	–	–	–
Nai	–	–	–	–	–	1	–	–	–	–	–	–	–	–
Dhanuk	–	–	–	–	–	1	1	–	–	1	–	1	2	–
Nuniya	–	–	–	–	–	–	–	1	1	–	–	–	–	–
Malah	–	–	–	–	–	–	–	–	–	–	1	–	–	–
Vishwakarma	–	–	–	–	–	–	–	–	–	–	1	–	–	–
Nishadh	–	–	–	–	–	–	–	–	–	–	–	1	1	–
TOTAL		**5**	**11**	**13**	**15**	**16**	**12**	**12**	**18**	**24**	**24**	**24**	**19**	**15**
Brahmin	8	7	8	5	7	4	5	5	3	4	2	2	6	4
Bhumihar	6	4	6	9	10	6	7	8	4	1	4	3	4	2
Rajput	12	13	10	7	4	8	10	9	8	4	6	6	6	7
Kayastha	4	4	–	2	–	3	–	1	3	1	1	2	2	–
TOTAL	**30**	**28**	**24**	**24**	**21**	**21**	**22**	**23**	**18**	**10**	**13**	**13**	**18**	**13**
Harijan	7	7	8	7	7	8	8	8	8	8	8	8	8	7
Adivasi	6	7	5	5	5	5	5	5	5	5	5	5	5	–
Muslim	3	3	2	2	3	2	5	6	3	6	4	6	3	4
Christian	–	–	–	–	–	1	1	–	1	1	1	1	1	1
Bengali	3	3	3	2	2	1	1	–	1	–	–	–	–	–
Grand Total	**55**	**53**	**53**	**53**	**53**	**54**	**54**	**54**	**54**	**54**	**54**	**54**	**54**	**40**

Source: Srikant (2005), *Bihar Mein Chunav,* Vani Prakashan, New Delhi, p. 37.

Appendix 5

Social Composition of President and Secretaries at the District Level in Bihar

Castes	RJD		Congress		BJP		SAMTA		CPI		CPI(M)	
	Number	Per cent	Number	Per cent	Number	Per cent	Number	Per cent	Number	Per cent	Number	Per cent
Bhumihar	1	2.04	6	41.61	10	17.24	5	12.17	12	26.66	5	14.70
Brahmin	–	–	7	15.7	10	17.24	2	4.87	5	11.11	1	2.94
Rajput	–	–	5	11.36	11	18.76	9	21.95	–	–	1	2.94
Kayasth	–	–	2	5.54	1	1.72	–	–	–	–	1	2.94
Yadav	18	36.73	4	9.09	3	5.17	2	4.87	6	13.13	5	2.94
Kurmi	1	2.04	2	4.54	4	6.37	4	9.75	3	6.66	2	14.70
Koeri	2	4.08	–	–	1	1.72	8	19.51	3	6.66	4	5.88
Muslim	13	26.53	7	15.90	–	–	1	2.43	2	4.44	2	11.76
SC	4	8.16	3	6.81	2	3.44	2	4.87	2	4.44	4	5.88
ST	1	2.4	2	5.54	1	1.72	–	–	3	6.66	4	11.76
Baniya	6	12.24	4	9.09	11	18.96	1	2.43	1	2.22	2	11.76
Bengali	–	–	–	–	–	–	–	–	1	2.22	2	5.88
Kharwar	–	–	–	–	–	–	–	–	1	2.22	–	5.88
Malaha	1	2.04	1	2.27	–	–	–	–	–	–	–	–
Kahar	–	–	–	–	–	–	1	2.43	–	–	–	–
Lohar	–	–	–	–	1	1.72	–	–	–	–	–	–
Panjabi	–	–	–	–	2	3.44	–	–	–	–	–	–
Paneri	–	–	–	–	–	–	1	2.43	–	–	–	–
Danuk	–	–	–	–	–	–	2	4.87	–	–	–	–
Turha	1	2.04	–	–	–	–	–	–	–	–	–	–
Not Availlable	1	2.04	1	2.27	1	1.72	3	7.31	6	13.12	1	2.94
Total	**49**		**44**		**58**		**41**		**45**		**34**	

Source: Prasann Kumar Chaudhary and Srikant (2001), *Bihar Mein Samajik Parivartan Ke Kuchh Ayam,* p. 332, Vani Prakashan, New Delhi.

Appendix 6

Caste of Candidates for Bihar Assembly Elections, 1995

	Janata Dal	*Congress*	*BJP*	*Samata Party*	*BPP*
Yadav	87	33	23	11	22
	(33.85)	(10.18)	(7.16)	(4.26)	(7,40)
Rajput	19	44	44	26	55
	(7.39)	(13.58)	(13.70)	(10.07)	(18.51)
Bhumihar	4	41	41	23	46
	(1.55)	(12.65)	(12.77)	(8.91)	(15.48)
Brahmin	4	37	29	16	22
	(1.55)	(11.41)	(9.03)	(6.20)	(7.40)
Kayastha	2	4	6	5	7
	(0.77)	(1.23)	(1.86)	(1.93)	(2.35)
Kurmi	11	15	16	45	17
	(4.28)	(4.62)	(4.98)	(17.44)	(5.72)
Koeri	19	6	15	36	14
	(7.39)	(1.85)	(4.67)	(13.95)	(4.71)
Muslims	33	42	1	37	29
	(12.84)	(12.96)	(0.31)	(14.34)	(9.76)
Christians	38	29	72	39	15
OBC	(14.78)	(8.95)	(22.42)	(15.11)	(5.05)
SC and ST	40	73	73	20	30
	(15.56)	(22.53)	(22.74)	(7.75)	(10.10)
Total	**257**	**322**	**321**	**258**	**297**
	(17.63)	**(22.23)**	**(22.03)**	**(17.70)**	**(20.38)**

Source: A.K. Lal, *Journal of Social and Economic Studies*, Vol. 13, 1996, p. 90.

Appendix 7

Caste Background of Chairmen, Members of Zila Parishads and Mukhias in Bihar 2001

(*In percentage*)

Caste Groups	*Chairmen*	*Members*	*Mukhias*
Upper Caste Hindus	35.2	25.3	34.0
(i) Brahmin	8.2	5.0	7.7
(ii) Bhumihar	13.5	9.1	12.1
fiii) Rajput	13.5	10.3	13.4
(iv) Kayastha	0.9	0.8	
Middle caste Hindus	45.9	42.1	45.7
(a) Annexure 1 castes	2.7	3.5	3.9
(i) Dhanuk		0.5	0.6
(ii) Mallah/Gorhi		1.2	2.0
(iii) Others	2.7	1.8	1.3
(b) Annexure II castes	43.2	39.6	41.8
(i) Yadav	35.1	24.2	24.2
(ii) Kurmi	2.7	4.1	5.8
(iii) Koeri		5.2	6.3
(iv) Baniavaishya	5.4	4.4	3.6
(v) Others		1.7	1.9
Scheduled Caste Hindus		16.9	1.06
(i) Dusadh		5.6	0.7
(ii) Dhobi		0.9	0.07
(iii) Pasi		1.2	0.05
(iv) Musahar		0.8	0.2
(v) Others		8.5	0.04
Scheduled Tribes		0.6	0.5
Muslims	16.2	13.0	15.6
Marwari	2.7	0.3	
Others	0.8	2.9	
Total	100.0	100.0	100.0
Chairmen/Members (N. Area)	37	1,160	7,120

Source: Saibal Gupta, "New Panchayat and Subaltern Resurgence." *Economic and Political Weekly*, Vol. 36, No. 29, July 2001.

Appendix 8

Position in Some Important Centres in Bihar

	Brahmin	*Bhumihar*	*Rajput*	*Kayastha*	*Yadava*	*Kurmi*	*Koeri*	*Bainia*	*Muslims*	*SC*	*ST*	*MBC*
Bihar Public Service Commission		1	1		1(Ch)	1	1	1	1	1	1	1
University Service Commission			1				1	1	1(Ch)			
College service Commission			1		1		1(Ch)		1	1	1	1
Inter Council			1	1(Ch)	1				1	1	1	
School Service Commission				1	1(Ch)	1					1	1
Vice-Chancellors	1		2			1			1	1		
Pro-Vice-Chancellors						2			2			
Registrars						2						
Poly/Med./.Eng Admn. Comm.						3						
College Principals	7	5	11	5		5	4	6	8	7	4	11
State Pollution Control Board						1						
Total	**8**	**6**	**17**	**7**	**4**	**16**	**8**	**8**	**15**	**11**	**8**	**14**

Source: Dr. Ranjan Yadav quoted in *Hindustan Times* on 9-11-1994. Analysed by Kumar Abhishek.

Note: Ch = Chairpersons.

Appendix 9

Caste and Community of Members of Janta Dal Governments in Bihar

Castes	*Lalu Prasad Yadav 1990-1995*	*Rabri Devi 1995-2000*
Upper Castes	26.7	17.1
Brahmin	N.A.	2.63
Rajputs	N.A	11.84
Bhumihar	N.A.	2.63
Upper OBC	35.2	51.31
Yadav	N.A.	31.58
Kurmi	N.A.	2.63
Keori	N.A.	11.84
Bania	N.A.	5.26
Lower OBC	11.3	6.58
SC/ST	15.5	13.16
Muslim	11.3	11.84
Total	**100 (N = 71)**	**100 (N = 76)**

Source: S.N. Chaudhary (1999), *Power-dependence Relations for Hegemony in Rural Bihar*, Har-Anand Publications, New Delhi, pp. 219, 251.

Index

Administrative power system, 32
Administrative structure, 24, 32
Agrarian reforms, 18
Agricultural labourers, 10–11, 20
Ahir-Koeri-Kurmi Syndicate, 43
Ahir-Kurmi-Koeri party, 79
All-India Kurmi Mahasabha, 40
Anti-Brahmin movements, 46
Apex-bottom power relations, 109
Aspirations, 2, 7, 11, 16, 35–36, 41, 47, 50–51, 72, 90–91, 105
  aroused, 4
  identical, 33
  local, 88
  psychological, 64
Awadhia Kurmis, 40

Backward Classes Commission, 51, 54, 58, 76, 115
Backwardness, 4, 47, 52–54, 56, 62, 66
  educational, 53
  identification of, 53–54
  measure, 63
  social, 10, 56, 63
  socio-economic, 81
Beneficiaries, 11, 53, 111
Bhagalpur University, 26
Bhumihars, 17, 23, 26, 74–75, 80, 84, 101–3
  dominance, 17, 74
Bhumihar Brahman College, 24
Bihar and Orissa Provincial Civil Service, 55
Bihar Chhatra Sangharsh Samiti, 84
Bihar Communism, 74
Bihar ownership, 19
Bihar Pradesh Congress Committee, 73
Bihar Pradesh Kisan Sabha, 17
Bihar Pradesh Kisan Sangh, 21
Bihar Provincial Congress Committee, 71
Bihar State Legislative Assembly, 117
BJP, 90, 92–93, 103
Brahmanic ideology of privilege scriptural, 32
Brahmin
  officials, 30
  organisation, 32
  orthodoxy, 33
British administration, 50
Bureaucracy, 3, 16, 18, 25, 34, 50, 53, 55, 76, 91, 111
  politics, 2
  state, 17, 55, 57–58
Bureaucrats, 8

Capitalist kulaks, new, 82
Caste
  associations, 23–24, 34, 37–41, 44, 107

bias, 102
class, 67
clusters, 63
coalitions, 75
cohesion, 96
composition, 26, 117–18
consciousness, 39
hierarchy, 2, 18, 31, 37–38, 41–42, 49–50, 52, 67, 72, 95, 97, 108
historians, 40
identity, 100
inequality, 73, 77
leaders, 23, 25
linkages, 36
mobility, 41
movements, 36
orientation, 44
origins, 63
pattern, 88
polarisation, 26
reservation, 52–53
artisan, 15, 58
ascendant, 67
assertive, 62, 65
criminal, 39
depressed, 11
deprived, 97
forward, 20
literate, 35
lower, 14–15, 20–21, 24–26, 30–31, 37, 39, 41–43, 45-46, 64–66, 72–74, 76, 80–82, 85–86, 103–5, 107–8
non-literate, 29
peasant, 3, 29
privileged, 55
rural, 45
superior, 91, 95–96
weaker, 96
solidarity, 41
status, 19, 52
war, 68
Casteism, 43, 78
Coalition Government, 79
Colonial administration, 23, 31–32, 35–36
Communist Party, 56, 74, 90
Congress Party, 18, 23, 30, 33, 42–43, 56, 71–72, 75–76, 78–81, 83, 85–86, 92, 98, 103–5, 108
Congress Socialist Party, 73

Educational attainment, 45
Euphemism, administrative, 10
Exploitative tradition, 49

Harijans, 17
Harvesting season, 21
Hegemonic structure, 67
Helplessness, 52
Heterogeneity, 26
Hierarchical dominance, 46
Hindi belt, 58
Hinduism, 62
Hindu Mythology, 40
Hindu rituals, 30, 37
Hindutva, 93
Homogenous communities, 63

Identical strategies, 37
Ideological stirrings, 1
International Labour Organisation, 26

Janata Government, 57–58
Janata Party, 58, 83, 85–86, 101
JP movement, 84–85

Kalelkar Commission, 55, 58
Kisan movement, 41
Kisan Sabha, 17, 73
Koeris, 17, 20, 22, 26, 40, 42, 69, 91–93, 96, 99–100, 102–3
Koeri Hitkari Sabha, 40
Kshatriyas, 38–40
Kumar, Nitish, 89, 91–92, 100
Kurmi caste association, 39

Kurmi leaders, 56

Land Ceiling Act, 18
Land control, 19
Landed aristocracy, 16
Landless, 11, 35
  households, 22
  labourers, 11, 16–19, 42, 61, 73, 111
Landlessness, 12
Landlordism, 73
Landowners, 11, 20
Land owning, 34
Land reforms, 11, 18
  measures, 18–19
Leadership, 1, 3, 16–17, 21, 25–26, 30–33, 36, 40, 42–43, 59, 71–75, 77–79, 82, 90, 104–5
  charishmatic, 94
  collective, 79
  structure, 26
  unquestioned, 104
Leaders of eminence, 23, 74
Legitimacy, 60–61, 106, 110
Lingayats, 33
Locus of Power, 88
Lopsided empowerment, 111
Lower caste families, 14

Mandal Commission, 26, 58–60, 63, 67, 91, 93, 95, 104
Mandalisation of politics, 100
Manipulation of caste, 110
Marginalisation, 89, 94, 96
Merit attention, 73
Middle peasants, 20
Middle range castes, 1–7, 11–13, 16–17, 19–23, 25–26, 37, 41–45, 54–58, 68–69, 72–74, 76–82, 84–86, 88–101, 103–4, 108–11
Mobility, 1, 3, 29, 37
  aspirations, 62, 65
  strategies, 45
Monopoly, 37
Mungeri Lal Commission, 59, 81, 86, 98
Muslim community, 92, 102
Muslim vote, 98
Mysore Princely State, 32

Nationalist movement, 32
National leadership, 10
National unity, 53, 72
Natural leaders, 44
Naxalite movement, 21, 86
Neutral administrative tools, 64–65
Non-Bhumihar, 74
Non-Brahmanical movement, 3, 36
Non-Brahmanism, 29, 35
Non-Brahmin castes, 33
Non-Brahmin strategies, 55
Non-Communist parties, 85
Non-Congress parties, 78

Panchayati Raj Institutions, 99
Para-communities, 6–8, 32
Party dominance, 26, 64, 71, 82, 88, 98, 108
Party leadership, 56
Peasants, 15–17, 19, 41–42, 61, 73
  affluent, 71
  impoverished, 72
  land owning, 21
  lower caste, 15
  middle caste, 4
  owner, 11
  poor, 20, 73
Peasant mobilisation problems, 21
Peasantry, 21, 73
Policy content, 66
Political
  alignments, 88
  ambitions, 72
  awakening, 82
  collaboration, 107
  consequences, 5
  developments, 4, 31, 82–83
  dividends, 90–91, 93

entrepreneur, 60
federation, 109
forces, 100
instability, 80, 84
investments, 92
modernisation, 7, 44, 101, 109
movements, 72
opponents, 83
outfits, 77
parties, 7, 22, 41, 44, 59–60, 72–73, 78, 98, 100, 102
pay-off, 92
pragmatism, 60
rehabilitation, 5, 81
renaissance, 5, 88
representation, 5, 103
space, 92
supremacy, 81
survival, 93
weakness, 49

Politics
appendage, 88
clientistic, 85, 105
contemporary, 103, 105
democratic, 42
factional, 71
lower caste, 44
mandalisation of, 4, 91
national, 44
patronage, 64
permissive, 83

Post-Independence phase, 18, 44

Power
civil, 83
democratic, 83
dispersal of, 51, 97, 100
institutions of, 8, 23, 96
locus of, 3, 30, 67, 69, 71, 95, 97

Power distribution, uneven, 96

Power structure, 4–5, 7, 12, 44, 51, 53, 72, 75, 78, 80, 82, 88, 95–97, 99–101, 109–10

Preferential programmes, 54

Priority attention, 102

Privileges, 14–15, 19, 24–25, 29, 37, 51, 55, 82, 108, 110
economic, 111
exclusive, 111
social, 41

Professional civil services, 62

Protective discrimination, 2, 49, 61–62, 64–66

Protest movement, 84, 108

Radical land reform, 59

Radical socio-economic programmes, 33

Rashtriya Janata Dal, 93, 100, 109

Reservation
benefits, 50, 59
caste-based, 53
denied, 34
extension of, 4, 64
favoured, 43
institutionalise, 58
policy, 57–58, 63
scheme, 64

Ritual
dominance, 1, 32
inferiority, 38
rank, 10, 109–10

Samata Party, 92–93, 98, 102–3

Samayukta Socialist Party, 74, 78–79

Sanskritisation, 41–42, 76

Satya Sodhak Samaj, 30–31

Savarna caste, 37

Self-help groups (SHGs), 34

Self-Respect Movement, 32

Sharecroppers, 19, 73, 111

Shudra politics, 44

Sinha, Satyendra Narain, 85

Social change, 4–5, 30, 68, 95

Social identities, 100

Social inequality, 108

Socialist parties, 75

Socialist Party, 78, 80

Socialist permutations, 77
Socialist programmes, 53
Social movements, 29, 45
Social order, 1, 3–4, 8, 30, 35, 44, 51, 109, 111
  exploitative, 46
  legitimised, 7
  traditional, 15, 49, 551
Social Reform Movement, 32
Social scientists, 3, 5, 53, 62
Socio-administrative resources, 107
Socio-economic dominance, 39
Sociological attention, 3
Socio-political constituency, 110
Socio-political unity, 6
Sponsored politicization, 4
State politics, 33, 81, 95, 103, 109
State protection, 62–63
Stratification system, 1–2, 12–15, 42, 95
Student movement, 84
Superior-inferior syndrome, 44
Support peasant movements, 16

Thakur, Karpoori, 59, 69, 74, 79, 82, 85, 98
Traditional stratification system, 1, 3, 6, 10, 35, 38, 44, 46, 107, 109–10
Transfer of power, 110

Unnatural dominance, 50, 77
Upper caste
  angry, 39
  bureaucracy, 57, 62
  control, 99
  elites, 80, 82, 86
  feudals, 11
  landlords, 21
  legislators, 85
  peasantry, 95
  values, 37

Vaishnavism, 37

Weighted index of backwardness, 4

Yadav, Lalu Prasad, 88–94, 96–100, 104
Yadav, Ram Lakhan Singh, 25, 75–76
Yadava caste association, 38

Zamindari, 16, 18
Zila Parishads, 99, 121